Paper Piecing
all year round

Mix & Match 24 Blocks
7 Projects to Sew

Mary Hertel

C&T PUBLISHING

Text copyright © 2020 by Mary Hertel

Photography and artwork copyright © 2020 by C&T Publishing, Inc.

Publisher: Amy Barrett-Daffin

Creative Director: Gailen Runge

Acquisitions Editor: Roxane Cerda

Managing Editor: Liz Aneloski

Editor: Katie Van Amburg

Technical Editor: Linda Johnson

Cover/Book Designer: April Mostek

Production Coordinator: Tim Manibusan

Production Editor: Alice Mace Nakanishi

Illustrator: Linda Johnson

Photo Assistant: Lauren Herberg

Photography by Estefany Gonzalez of C&T Publishing, Inc., unless otherwise noted

Published by C&T Publishing, Inc., P.O. Box 1456, Lafayette, CA 94549

Library of Congress Cataloging-in-Publication Data

Names: Hertel, Mary, 1955- author.

Title: Paper piecing all year round : mix & match 24 blocks : 7 projects to sew / Mary Hertel.

Description: Lafayette, CA : C&T Publishing, 2020.

Identifiers: LCCN 2020024669 | ISBN 9781617458941 (trade paperback) | ISBN 9781617458958 (ebook)

Subjects: LCSH: Patchwork--Patterns. | Sewing.

Classification: LCC TT835 .H4468 2020 | DDC 746.46/041--dc23

LC record available at https://lccn.loc.gov/2020024669

Printed in the USA

10 9 8 7 6 5 4 3 2 1

Dedication I dedicate this book to my special friends, Jan, Shelley, and Pauline, who are always willing to test patterns, give design advice, and concoct crazy names for my many patterns. Their support means so much to me.

Acknowledgments Thank you to the amazing editors at C&T Publishing. You make the book writing process so easy!

Contents

*January
Snowman 1   39*

*January
Snowman 2   40*

*February
Valentine with
Bow   41*

*February
Valentine with
Arrow   42*

*March
Gnome with Fish   43*

*March
Gnome with Flower   44*

*April
Bunny in a
Flower Pot   45*

*April
Chick in a
Flower Pot   46*

*May
Butterfly Profile   47*

*May
Butterfly   48*

*June
Watering Can   49*

*June
Tulips   50*

*July
Patriotic Pup
with Glasses   51*

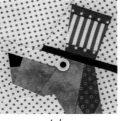

*July
Patriotic Pup
with Hat   52*

*August
Crab   53*

*August
Octopus   54*

*September
Acorns   55*

*September
Squirrel   56*

*October
Cat with Bow Tie   57*

*October
Cat with Hat   58*

*November
Turkey with Hat   59*

*November
Turkey   60*

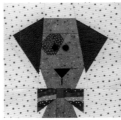

*December
Christmas Puppy   61*

*December
Christmas Puppy
with Hat   62*

About the
Author
63

Introduction

If you love seasonal decorating like I do, this book will make you smile. I have those special spots in my home where I enjoy adding a touch of the seasons, whether that be Spring, Summer, Fall, or Winter.

This book features 2 paper-pieced block designs for each month to use in the project of your choice. Decorate your home with quilts, mini quilts, hand towels, pillows, pot holders—and even decorate the baby with seasonal bibs!

Now, for the best part ... all 24 of these adorable blocks will fit in the projects made for 8″ × 8″ blocks from my previous books. So, not only can you create the five projects from this book, but also totes, table toppers, mug rugs, place mats, and so much more.

Sounds like fun—and let's get right to the fun by paper piecing these super-cute blocks. Everything you need to know, you will find right here!

Photo by Gail Cameron

Paper-Piecing Basics

Paper piecing is a simple, straightforward method of sewing a design into a project. Perhaps you have experienced the joy and satisfaction of seeing the finished image after adding the last piece to a jigsaw puzzle. The effects of paper piecing are no different. Anyone with basic sewing skills can master paper piecing, as the approach used in this book is essentially sewing by number. Paper piecing is also a creative means of using up oddly shaped pieces of fabric that might otherwise have been relegated to the scrap pile.

Tools

- Paper (I recommend Carol Doak's Foundation Paper by C&T Publishing.)
- Sharp scissors
- Rotary cutter and mat
- Ruler with an easy-to-read ¼" line (such as Add-A-Quarter ruler by CM Designs)
- Multiuse tool (such as Alex Anderson's 4-in-1 Essential Sewing Tool by C&T Publishing) or seam ripper
- Flat-head straight pins
- Lamp or natural light source
- Sewing machine
- Iron and pressing board

Things to Know

STITCH LENGTH

Set the stitch length on your machine to 1.5, which is about 20 stitches per inch. When paper piecing, the stitch perforations must be close together to allow the paper to rip easily, but not so close that ripping out a seam is an impossible task.

PREPARE A CONVENIENT WORK STATION

Have the iron, pressing board, and cutting mat close to the sewing machine. There should be a light source handy for positioning scrap pieces on the back of the block pattern. A window works well during the day, and a lamp at night.

THE BUTTERFLY EFFECT

After sewing a seamline, the fabric is flipped behind the numbered piece that you are currently attaching. This creates a butterfly effect, meaning that the fabric scrap needs to be lined up to the seam in such a way that it will cover the space you are sewing after it is flipped into place. If you are concerned that the size of the scrap is insufficient, pin along the seamline and try flipping the scrap into place before sewing the seam. That way, if the scrap does not cover the area sufficiently, you can adjust it or find a larger scrap.

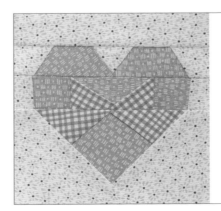

FOLLOW ALONG

If you are new to paper piecing, follow along for practice using the Valentine with Bow block (page 41) as you read the following instructions.

Preparing the Patterns

1 Make the recommended number of color copies of the original block. (You need 2 copies for the Valentine with Bow block.)

2 Cut the block into the segments denoted by the capital letters, *adding ¼" seam allowances along the red lines and the outside edges of the block.* For the example, use 1 copy for each of the Segments A and C, the other copy for Segment B.

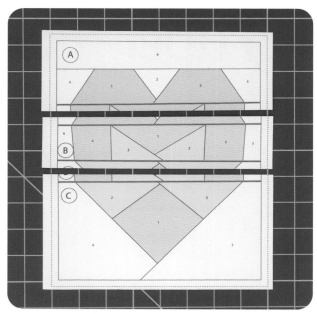

Segments A, B, and C with ¼" seam allowances around outside edges

Paper Piecing a Segment

Always stitch pieces in numerical order. Don't forget to set your stitch length (page 7) to 1.5, or about 20 stitches per inch.

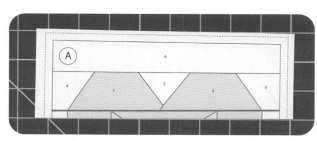

Front side of Segment A

1 Pin the *wrong* side of the Piece 1 fabric onto the *unprinted* side of the paper pattern. The right side of the fabric faces you (away from the paper).

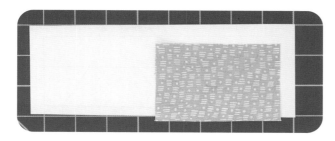

2 Bend the paper pattern and fabric along the seam-line between Pieces 1 and 2. (See arrow.) Use the side of a pencil or pressing tool (such as the presser cap on Alex Anderson's 4-in-1 Essential Sewing Tool), or a heavy piece of tagboard (such as a bookmark or postcard) to make the fold. (This will help you align the fabric for Piece 2.)

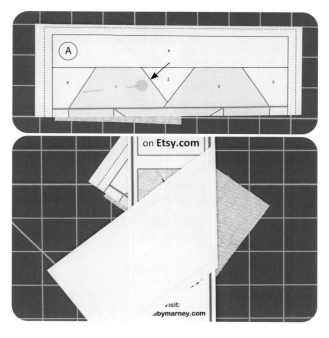

3 Use the Add-A-Quarter ruler to trim the fabric behind Piece 1 to ¼".

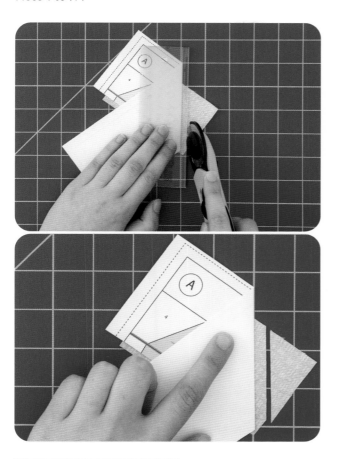

4 Keeping the pattern bent back along the seamline, align the Piece 2 fabric with the fabric from Piece 1. The fabric for Piece 2 will be flipped into place after sewing. Pin in place, right sides together.

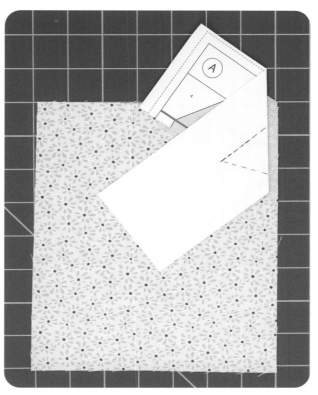

Tip: Right Sides Together   *As you are piecing, the right sides of fabric should always be together.*

5 Flip the pattern flat and sew ¼" beyond the seamline at the beginning and the end of this seam (as shown by the green line). No backtacking is needed, as the ends of the seams are stitched over by other seams. Notice that the fabric for Piece 2 is much larger than needed; it will be trimmed later.

Tip: Double-Check to Avoid Seam Ripping

I like to use large scraps (but no larger than 9″ × 11″) and trim the piece after sewing it in place. As you place the fabric under the presser foot to sew, the seam allowance and the shape you are filling should be to your right. The shape you previously completed should be to your left. Before sewing, do a mental check. Ask yourself these two questions: "Is the piece I am working on to my right?" and "Is the majority of my fabric to my left?" If the answer is yes, then sew. This simple check will eliminate much seam ripping.

6 Flip the fabric into position behind Piece 2 and press. Pin in place to keep it flat.

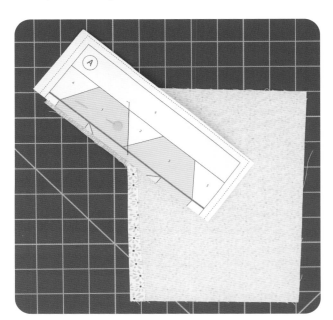

7 Trim the fabric a generous ½" beyond the remaining edges of Piece 2. *Do not cut the pattern.*

8 Continue to add the remaining pieces in the same manner as you added Piece 2.

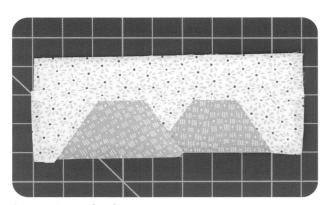

Segment A completed

Tip: Stitches Interfering?

Overstitching the seams may at times interfere with an exact fold along a stitching line. In this case, tear the paper just enough to release it from the stitching.

9 At the red line, trim the seam allowance of Segment A to an *exact* ¼″ seam. Use a rotary cutter, a mat, and a ruler with a ¼″ line.

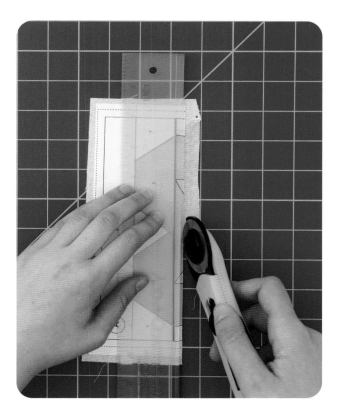

The segment is now ready to be sewn to the other segments. Follow the same process to make Segment B.

Joining Segments

Note: Make sure each segment is trimmed so that it has an exact ¼″ seam allowance along the red segment seamlines. Do not trim the outer edge seam allowances at this time.

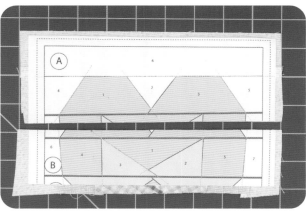

Segments have ¼″ seam allowances where they will be joined

1 With right sides together, pin together the edges of Segments A and B, matching the red sewing lines. Push a straight pin through the end of each red line to help align them as closely as possible. Sew on the red line and ¼″ past the red line on both ends.

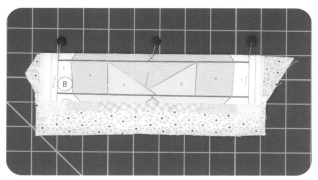

Sew segments together on red line.

2 Remove the paper from the seam allowance *only* to eliminate the possibility of the paper getting trapped under the seams.

3 Press the seam to a side. Let the seam "show" you in which direction it wants to be pressed.

> **Tip: Finish Before Trimming**
>
> *Make sure never to trim the excess fabric from the outer edges of the block until all block segments have been sewn together. Only then is it safe to square up the block using a cutting mat, ruler, and a rotary cutter.*

4 Complete any embroidery *while* the paper is still attached. (I use a running stitch with 6 strands of embroidery floss.) The paper acts as a stabilizer and will keep the block from stretching. *After* the block has been attached to the project, the paper may be removed. Follow the project instructions to know when buttons and embellishments are added.

Projects

Create five adorable projects
using any of the 24 paper-pieced blocks.
Any block works in any project.

Baby Quilt

FINISHED QUILT: 45″ × 31″

Materials

Fabric A: 1½ yards nondirectional fabric for main fabric and binding

Fabric B: ½ yard for sashing and paper-pieced block backgrounds

Fabric C: 1½ yards nondirectional fabric for backing

Assorted scraps: For paper piecing (See your selected block's materials list.)

Batting: 1 rectangle 53″ × 39″

Rickrack trim: 2 yards of 1″ wide

Felt: 3″ squares in black and/or white (*For baby's safety, substitute felt for buttons* only *if your selected block requires buttons.*)

Additional supplies: See block pattern for floss and so on.

Cutting

WOF = width of fabric

Fabric A

• Cut 1 rectangle 24½″ × 31″.

• Cut 1 rectangle 9½″ × 31″.

• Cut 4 strips 2½″ × WOF for binding.

Fabric B

• Cut 3 strips 2½″ × WOF. Subcut 1 strip into 4 sashing rectangles 2½″ × 8″.

Sewing

Use ¼″ seams throughout, unless otherwise directed.

PAPER-PIECED BLOCKS

Refer to Paper-Piecing Basics (page 7) as needed. Refer to Block Patterns (page 38) to choose blocks.

1 Paper piece 3 selected blocks, using Fabric B as the background fabric for each block and the assorted scraps for the rest of the block.

2 Add any necessary embroidery. Do not add buttons, but mark their placement if indicated.

3 Trim each block to 8″ × 8″.

ATTACH THE SASHING TO THE BLOCKS

1 Sew a Fabric B sashing rectangle 2½″ × 8″ to the top of each paper-pieced block. Press the seams towards the sashing.

Sew sashing to top of each block.

2 Sew the 3 paper-pieced blocks together into a vertical column. Press the seams toward the sashing.

3 Sew a Fabric B sashing rectangle 2½″ × 8″ to the bottom of the paper-pieced column. Press the seam toward the sashing.

4 Sew a Fabric B strip 2½″ × WOF to each side of the column. Press the seams towards the sashing strips.

5 Trim the excess fabric strips using a ruler and rotary cutter.

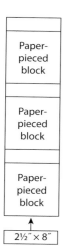

Sew sashing to bottom of column.

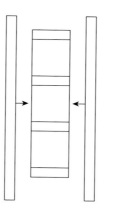 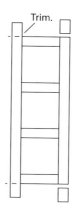

Sew sashing strip to column sides.

Trim excess strips.

ADD MAIN FABRIC SECTIONS

1 With right sides together, pin the smaller Fabric A rectangle 9½″ × 31″ to the left side of the paper-pieced column, matching the 31″ edges. Sew together. Press the seam toward the sashing strip.

2 With right sides together, pin the larger Fabric A rectangle 24½″ × 31″ to the right side of the paper-pieced column, matching the 31″ edges. Sew together. Press the seam toward the sashing strip.

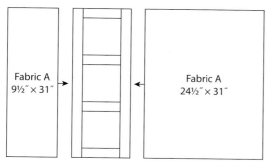

Main fabric attached to blocks

QUILTING

1 Remove the paper from the back of the paper-pieced blocks.

2 Layer the Fabric C backing (right side facing down), batting, and quilt top (right side facing up).

3 Pin all 3 layers together and quilt as desired.

ATTACH THE RICKRACK

1 Pin a 32″ length of 1″-wide rickrack over each main fabric seam, where the main fabric meets the sashing. Stitch down the center of the rickrack, through all layers.

2 Trim the edge of the rickrack even with the raw edge of the quilt.

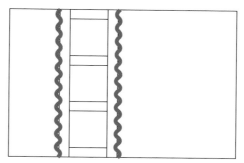

Attach rickrack.

BINDING

1 Pin together 2 Fabric A binding strips 2½″ × WOF, overlapping at a right (90°) angle, with right sides together. Mark a diagonal line from Corner A to Corner B. Sew on the diagonal line to connect the strips. Trim the seam to ¼″ and press the seams open. Continue, adding all 4 strips together in this manner to make 1 long, continuous strip for binding.

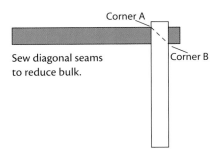

Sew diagonal seams to reduce bulk.

2 Press the binding strip in half lengthwise with wrong sides together.

3 Align the raw edges of the binding strip with the raw edges of the quilt. Bend the beginning of the strip at a right (90°) angle with the tail facing away from the quilt.

4 Stitch ¼″ from the raw edges. Stop stitching ¼″ from the first corner and backtack.

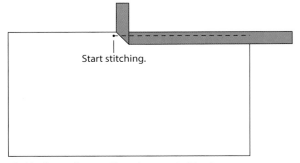

Start stitching.

Pin binding strip to quilt and start stitching here.

5 Fold the binding strip straight up. The raw edge of the binding strip should align with the raw edge of the second side of the quilt.

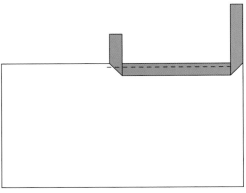

Starting first corner

6 Fold the binding strip straight down to overlap the second edge of the quilt. Start stitching at the top corner and continue until ¼″ from the next corner and backtack.

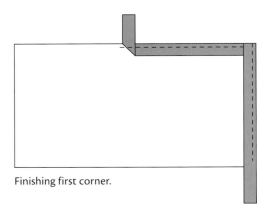

Finishing first corner.

7 Continue in this manner around the remaining sides of the quilt, backtacking and turning at each corner.

8 Trim the end of the binding strip so it overlaps the angled beginning section by 2″. Trim away the remaining tail.

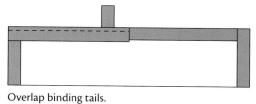

Overlap binding tails.

9 Press the binding around to the back of the quilt and hand stitch in place, easing in the fullness where the tails overlap.

FINISHING

If your chosen block indicates buttons, appliqué felt circles in place at this time instead of buttons.

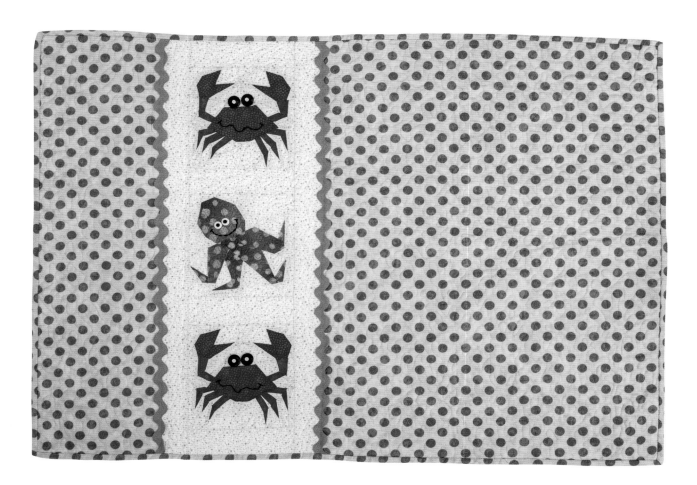

Mini Quilt Series

FINISHED QUILTS:
Mini Quilt: 8˝ × 8˝ • Mini Quilt with Checkerboard: 11½˝ × 14˝
Mini Quilt with Pinwheels: 12˝ × 13¾˝

Mini Quilt with Checkerboard (page 20)
*(For alternative designs, see Mini Quilt, page 19,
and Mini Quilt with Pinwheels, page 22.)*

Mini Quilt   Mini Quilt with Checkerboard   Mini Quilt with Pinwheels

Mini Quilt

FINISHED QUILT: 8˝ × 8˝

Materials

Makes 2 Mini Quilts.

Fabric A: ½ yard for backings, hangers, and binding

Materials for 2 blocks: See your selected blocks' materials lists.

Batting: 2 squares 9˝ × 9˝

Cutting

WOF = width of fabric

Fabric A

Cut in the order listed.

- Cut 2 strips 2½˝ × WOF for binding.

- Cut 2 squares 9˝ × 9˝ for backings.

- Cut 2 rectangles 2˝ × 7½˝ for hangers.

Mini Quilt Construction

Use ¼˝ seams throughout, unless otherwise directed.

PAPER-PIECED BLOCKS

Refer to Paper-Piecing Basics (page 7) as needed. Refer to Block Patterns (page 38) to choose 2 blocks.

1 Paper piece 2 selected blocks, using the fabrics listed in the blocks' materials lists. (Note that other mini quilts may provide background and paper-piecing fabrics. Read the materials lists carefully.)

2 Add any necessary embroidery to the blocks. Do not add buttons at this time, but mark their placement.

3 Trim the blocks to 8˝ × 8˝.

QUILTING

The remaining instructions apply to each of the 2 blocks.

1 Remove the paper from the back of the block.

2 Layer the Fabric A backing (right side facing down), batting, and mini quilt (right side facing up).

3 Pin all 3 layers together and quilt as desired.

BINDING

To make and attach the binding, follow the instructions in Baby Quilt, Binding (page 16), using the Fabric A binding strips.

ADDING HANGER

1 Press under ½″ on each 2″ side edge of the Fabric A rectangle 2″ × 7½″. Topstitch ¼″ from each 2″ side edge for the side hems.

2 Press under ½″ along the 7½″ edges.

3 Center and pin the hanger to the back of the mini quilt, right below the binding. Hand stitch along the top and bottom of the hanger, leaving the sides open.

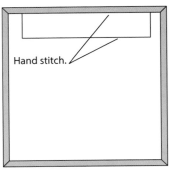

Placement of hanger

FINISHING

Hand stitch any desired buttons in place, sewing through all layers. Slide the hanger onto any 8″-wide mini quilt rack.

Mini Quilt with Checkerboard
FINISHED QUILT: 11½″ × 14″

Materials

Makes 2 Mini Quilts with Checkerboards.

Fabric A: (Red) ¼ yard for sashing

Fabric B: (Dark blue) ¾ yard for checkerboards, backings, hangers, and binding

Fabric C: (Blue dot on white) ¼ yard for checkerboards (Includes enough to paper piece block backgrounds.)

Assorted scraps: For paper piecing (See your selected block's materials list.)

Batting: 2 rectangles 13″ × 15″

Cutting

WOF = width of fabric. Fold fabric selvage to selvage. Complete all cutting before paper piecing the blocks.

Fabric A

- Cut 1 strip 2½″ × WOF. Subcut 4 rectangles 2½″ × 8″.

- Cut 2 strips 2¼″ × WOF. Subcut 4 rectangles 2¼″ × 12″ for sashing.

Fabric B

Cut in the order listed.

- Cut 3 strips 2½″ × WOF for binding.

- Cut 1 strip 1½″ × WOF for checkerboards.

- Cut 2 rectangles 16″ × 14″ for backings.

- Cut 2 rectangles 2″ × 10½″ for hangers.

Fabric C

- Cut 1 strip 1½″ × WOF for checkerboards.

- Use remaining fabric to paper piece block background.

Mini Quilt with Checkerboard Construction

Use ¼" seams throughout, unless otherwise directed.

PAPER-PIECED BLOCKS

1 Follow the instructions for Mini Quilt Construction under Paper-Pieced Blocks (page 19) to make 2 blocks.

ATTACH SASHING TO THE BLOCK

The remaining instructions apply to each of the 2 blocks.

1 Sew a Fabric A rectangle 2½" × 8" to the top and bottom of the paper-pieced block. Press the seams toward the sashing.

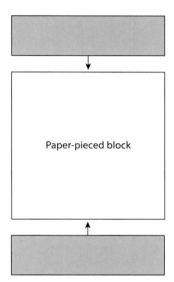

Sashing strips added to top and bottom of block

2 Sew a Fabric A rectangle 2¼" × 12" to each side of the paper-pieced block. Press the seams toward the sashing.

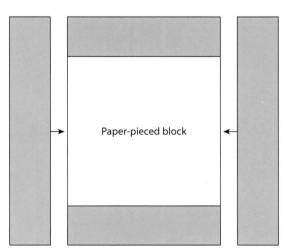

Sew sashing strips along sides of block.

PREPARE AND ATTACH THE CHECKERBOARD BOTTOM PANEL

1 Sew a 1½" × WOF Fabric B and Fabric C strip together along their lengthwise edges. Press the seam toward the darker fabric.

2 Cut the resulting strip into 22 units, each 1½" wide. This will be enough for 2 checkerboards.

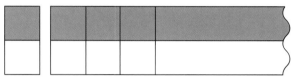

Cut units 1½" wide.

3 Using 11 of the units, sew 2 units together at a time, flipping so opposite colored fabrics will line up, like in a checkerboard. Press the seams open. There will be 5 checked four-patches and 1 remaining unit.

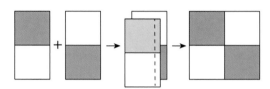

Sew 2 units together.

4 Sew the 5 four-patches together, side by side, to form a checkerboard. Sew the 1 remaining unit to the end. Press all seams open.

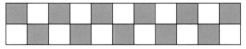

Make a checkerboard panel.

5 Sew the checkerboard panel to the mini quilt bottom. Press the seam toward the sashing.

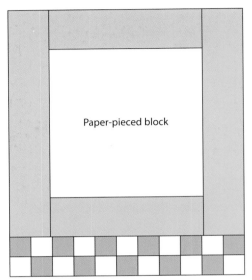

Checkerboard panel attached

QUILTING, BINDING, ADDING HANGER, AND FINISHING

Follow the instructions for Mini Quilt Construction under the separate heads Quilting, Binding, Adding Hanger, and Finishing (pages 19–20). Use the Fabric B rectangles 2″ × 10½″ for the hangers. Hang the finished mini quilts on 12″ × 14″ mini quilt hangers.

Mini Quilt with Pinwheels

FINISHED QUILT: 12″ × 13¾″

Materials

Makes 2 Mini Quilts with Pinwheels.

Fabric A: (Pink) ⅝ yard for sashing, backings, and hangers

Fabric B: (White) ¼ yard for pinwheels (Includes enough to paper piece, if your chosen block calls for it.)

Fabric C: (Blue dot) ¼ yard for pinwheels (Includes enough to paper piece block backgrounds.)

Fabric D: (Pink) ¼ yard for binding

Assorted scraps: For paper piecing (See your selected block's materials list.)

Batting: 2 rectangles 13″ × 15″

Cutting

WOF = width of fabric. Fold fabric selvage to selvage. Complete all cutting before paper piecing the blocks.

Fabric A

Cut in the order listed.

- Cut 1 strip 14″ × WOF. Subcut 2 rectangles 14″ × 16″ for backings.

- Cut 1 strip 2½″ × WOF. Subcut 4 rectangles 2½″ × 10″ for sashing.

- Cut 1 strip 2″ × WOF. Subcut 2 rectangles 2″ × 10½″ for hangers.

- Cut 1 strip 1½″ × WOF. Subcut 4 rectangles 1½″ × 8″ for sashing.

Fabric B

- Cut 1 strip 4″ × WOF. Subcut 6 squares 4″ × 4″ for pinwheels.

- Depending on your choice of block, use remainder for paper piecing.

Fabric C

- Cut 1 strip 4″ × WOF. Subcut 6 squares 4″ × 4″ for pinwheels.

- Use remaining fabric to paper piece block background.

Fabric D

- Cut 3 strips 2½″ × WOF for binding.

Mini Quilt with Pinwheels Construction

Use ¼" seams throughout, unless otherwise directed.

PAPER-PIECED BLOCKS

1 Follow the instructions for Mini Quilt Construction under Paper-Pieced Blocks (page 19) to make 2 blocks.

ATTACH SASHING TO THE BLOCK

The following instructions apply to each of the 2 blocks.

1 Sew a Fabric A rectangle 1½" × 8" to the top and bottom of the paper-pieced block. Press the seams toward the sashing.

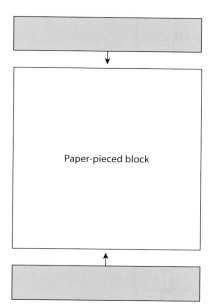

Add sashing strips to top and bottom of block.

2 Sew a Fabric A strip 2½" × 10" to each side of the paper-pieced block. Press the seams toward the sashing.

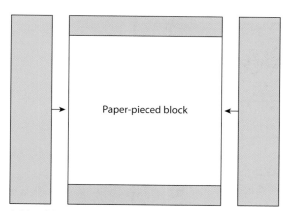

Add sashing strips to either side.

PREPARE 3 PINWHEELS

1 Match a Fabric B and a Fabric C square 4" × 4", right sides together. Sew all the way around the squares, staying ¼" from the edge.

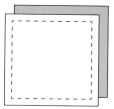

Sew 2 squares together.

2 Cut the sewn squares on the diagonal in both directions. There will be 4 resulting pieces.

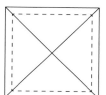

Cut squares into 4 pieces.

3 Open the 4 pieces, pressing the seam toward the darker fabric.

4 Lay out the 4 half-square triangles to form a pinwheel.

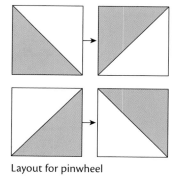

Layout for pinwheel

5 Sew the top row pinwheels together. Repeat with the bottom row pinwheels. Press the seams open.

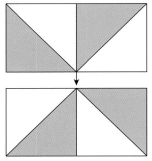

Sew pinwheels together in rows.

6 Sew the top and bottom rows together. Press the seams open.

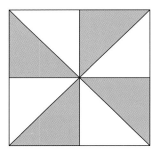

7 Repeat Steps 1–6 for the remaining 2 pinwheels. Trim the 3 finished pinwheels to 4¼″ × 4¼″, if they are not already at that size.

ATTACH THE PINWHEEL PANEL TO THE MINI QUILT

1 Sew the 3 pinwheels side by side in a horizontal row. Press the seams open.

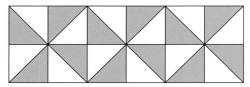

Make a pinwheel panel.

2 Sew pinwheel panel to the bottom of the mini quilt. Pin the panel at both ends to the prepared block first, then pin at the center. Ease any fullness while sewing the seam. Press the seam toward the sashing.

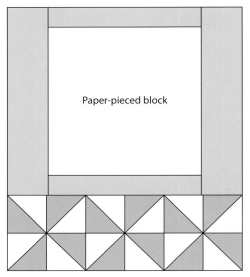

Paper-pieced block

Attach pinwheels to bottom.

QUILTING, BINDING, ADDING HANGER, AND FINISHING

Follow the instructions for Mini Quilt Construction under the separate heads Quilting, Binding, Adding Hanger, and Finishing (pages 19–20). Use the Fabric D strips 2½″ × WOF for binding, and the Fabric A rectangles 2″ × 10½″ for the hangers. Hang the finished mini quilts on 12″ × 14″ mini quilt hangers.

Pillow

FINISHED PILLOW: 19˝ × 19˝

Materials

Fabric A: 1 yard for main fabric

Fabric B: 1 fat eighth (9″ × 21″) for inner border

Materials for 2 blocks: See your selected blocks' materials lists.

Muslin: ⅔ yard for lining

Batting: 1 square 23″ × 23″

Pillow form: 18″ × 18″

Additional supplies: See block pattern for buttons, floss, and so on.

Felt (*optional*): 3″ squares in black and/or white (*For baby's safety:* If this pillow is to be used for a baby, substitute felt for buttons *only* if your selected block requires buttons.)

Cutting

WOF = width of fabric

Fabric A

• Cut 1 strip 19½″ × WOF. Subcut 2 rectangles 13½″ × 19½″ for pillow back and 2 squares 8″ × 8″ for pillow front.

• Cut 2 strips 2″ × WOF. Subcut *each* strip into 2 strips 2″ × 17½″ and 2″ × 20½″ for outer border.

Fabric B

• Cut 4 strips 1½″ × WOF (the 21″ length). Subcut 2 strips 1½″ × 15½″ and 2 strips 1½″ × 17½″ for inner border.

Muslin

• Cut 1 square 23″ × 23″ for lining.

Sewing

Use a ¼″ seam allowance throughout, unless otherwise directed.

PAPER-PIECED BLOCKS

Refer to Paper-Piecing Basics (page 7) as needed. Refer to Block Patterns (page 38) to choose blocks.

1 Paper piece 2 selected blocks.

2 Add any necessary embroidery to the blocks. Do not add any buttons at this time, but mark their placement.

3 Trim each block to 8″ × 8″.

CONSTRUCT THE PILLOW FRONT

1 Sew 1 Fabric A square 8″ × 8″ to the right of the first paper-pieced block and 1 to the left of the second paper-pieced block. Press the seams toward the squares.

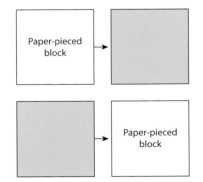

Fabric squares sewn to paper-pieced blocks

2 With right sides together, sew the top section to the bottom section, matching the center seams.

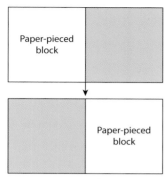

Sew top section to bottom section.

ATTACH THE INNER BORDER

1 Sew the shorter Fabric B strips 1½″ × 15½″ to the top and bottom of the paper-pieced unit. Press the seams toward the borders.

2 Sew the longer Fabric B strips 1½″ × 17½″ to the sides of the paper-pieced unit. Press the seams toward the borders.

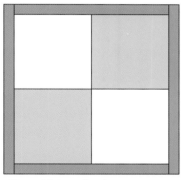

Pillow with inner borders

ATTACH THE OUTER BORDER

1 Sew the shorter Fabric A strips 2″ × 17½″ to the top and bottom of the pillow. Press the seams toward the outer border.

2 Sew the longer Fabric A strips 2″ × 20½″ to the sides of the pillow. Press the seams toward the outer border. The front of the pillow is oversized to allow for trimming after the quilting is finished.

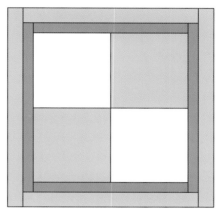

Pillow with outer borders

PREPARE THE PILLOW BACK

1 Press one long 19½″ edge of 2 Fabric A rectangles 13½″ × 19½″ under ½″. Press under another ½″ on the same edges. Stitch ⅜″ from the hemmed edges (or as close to the pressed-under edge as possible).

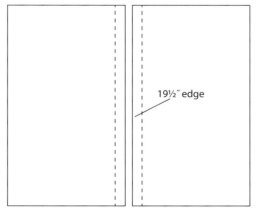

Hem pillow back pieces.

2 With the right sides facing down, place the rectangles on top of each other, overlapping the hemmed edges 5″. Pin the 2 pieces together where they overlap. The piece should measure 19½″ × 19½″. Adjust if needed.

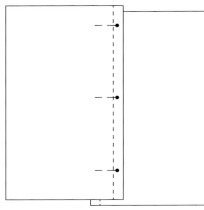

Overlap 5″ and pin together.

QUILTING

1 Remove the paper from the back of the paper-pieced blocks.

2 Layer the muslin lining (there is no right or wrong side to muslin), batting, and pillow font (right side facing up). Pin all 3 layers together, and quilt as desired.

3 Trim the quilted unit to 19½″ × 19½″.

4 Hand sew any buttons in place. Or if this pillow is to be used for a baby, appliqué fabric or felt circles in place instead of using buttons, which might be a choking hazard.

ASSEMBLE THE PILLOW

1 With right sides together, pin the quilted pillow front to the prepared pillow back.

2 Sew around all 4 sides using a ¼″ seam allowance.

3 Turn the pillow right side out through the opening in the pillow. Use a blunt tool to gently poke the corners square. Press the edges flat.

4 Topstitch ½″ from all 4 edges of the pillow.

5 Insert the 18″ × 18″ pillow form.

Hand Towel

FINISHED TOWEL:
7½″ wide × 20″ long

Materials

Makes 1 towel.

Fabric A: ¼ yard for backing and lining

Muslin: ⅓ yard

Paper-pieced block: See your selected block's materials list.

Fusible fleece: ¼ yard

Hand towel: 1 approximately 20″ wide × 28″ long
(This will be enough for 2 towels.)

Fasteners: 2 snaps or buttons, ⅝″ diameter

Additional supplies: See block pattern for buttons, floss, and so on.

Cutting

WOF = width of fabric

Fabric A

Fold fabric selvage to selvage.

• Cut 1 strip, 8″ × WOF. Subcut 1 square 8″ × 8″ for backing and 1 rectangle 8″ × 15½″ for lining.

Muslin

• Cut 1 rectangle 9″ × 16½″.

Fusible fleece

• Cut 1 rectangle 8″ × 15½″.

Sewing

Use ¼″ seams throughout, unless otherwise directed.

PAPER-PIECED BLOCK

Refer to Paper-Piecing Basics (page 7) as needed. Refer to Block Patterns (page 38) to choose a block.

1 Paper piece 1 selected block.

2 Add any necessary embroidery. Do not add any buttons at this time, but mark their placement.

3 Trim the block to 8″ × 8″.

CONSTRUCT THE TOWEL HANGER FRONT

1 Sew the Fabric A backing square 8″ × 8″ to the top of the paper-pieced block, right sides together. Press the seam toward Fabric A.

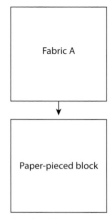

Sew backing square to top of paper-pieced block.

2 Remove the paper from the back of the paper-pieced block.

3 Steam press the 8″ × 15½″ fusible fleece to the back of the paper-pieced block unit.

4 Pin the muslin rectangle 9″ × 16½″ to the back of the fusible fleece.

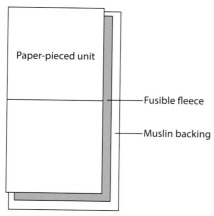

Paper-pieced unit

Fusible fleece

Muslin backing

Layer pieces for quilting.

5 Quilt as desired. Trim away excess muslin.

6 Hand stitch any desired buttons in place.

LINE THE TOWEL HANGER

1 Press the 8″ backing end of the quilted unit under ¼″. Do the same along an 8″ edge of the lining.

Back of quilted unit

Back of Fabric A lining

Pressed hems

2 Pin the Fabric A lining over the front of the quilted hanger, right sides together. The pressed-under edges should be lined up to each other.

3 Leaving the pressed-under edge open, stitch around 3 sides through all layers, backtacking at the beginning and end.

Sew around 3 sides.

4 Trim the corner seam allowances. Turn the hanger right sides out. Use a dowel to poke the corners square. Press.

ATTACH THE TOWEL

1 Cut the hand towel in half widthwise. (The second half may be saved for making another hand towel if you wish.) Finish the cut edge with a small zigzag stitch. Gather the cut end with a basting stitch, or fold into small pleats so it will fit inside the 7½″ open end of the towel hanger. Pin in place inside the open end of the hanger.

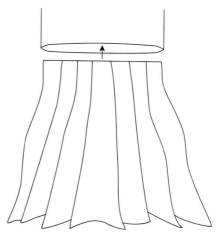

Gather towel to fit.

2 Stitch through all thickness ⅛″ from the open end, being careful to catch the pressed hem in the back in the stitching. Stitch again ¼″ from the first seam.

ATTACH FASTENERS

Option 1: Snaps

Attach snaps 1″ from the corners of the hanger. The female pieces will be under the bottom edge of the paper-pieced block; the male pieces will be close to the corners where the towel was attached.

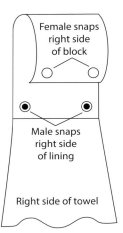

Female snaps right side of block

Male snaps right side of lining

Right side of towel

Snap placement

Option 2: Buttons

Sew buttonholes 1″ from the bottom edge of the paper-pieced block, and sew buttons to the corners above the towel stitching.

Baby Bib

FINISHED BIB: 9″ × 16″

Materials

Fabric A: ¼ yard for sashing and paper piecing block background

Fabric B: ¼ yard *or* 1 fat quarter for bib top

Fabric C: ⅓ yard for lining (Fleecy fabric is recommended.)

Assorted scraps: For paper piecing (See your selected block's materials list.)

Hook-and-loop tape: 1″ square

Felt: 2 squares 3″ each in black and/or white. (*For baby's safety*, substitute felt for buttons *only* if your selected block requires buttons.)

Additional supplies: See block pattern for floss and so on.

Cutting

WOF = width of fabric

Fabric A

- Cut 1 rectangle 4½″ × 10″.

- Cut 1 strip 1½″ × WOF. Subcut 2 rectangles 1½″ × 8″.

- Use remaining fabric to paper piece block background.

Fabric B

- Using the Baby Bib Top pattern (page 37), cut 1 bib top.

Fabric C

- Cut 1 rectangle 12″ × 24″.

Sewing

Use ¼″ seams throughout, unless otherwise directed.

PAPER-PIECED BLOCK

Refer to Paper-Piecing Basics (page 7) as needed. Refer to Block Patterns (page 38) to choose a block.

1 Paper piece 1 selected block.

2 Add any necessary embroidery. Do not add buttons, but mark their placement if indicated.

3 Trim the block to 8″ × 8″.

CONSTRUCT THE FRONT OF THE BIB

1 Sew the Fabric A strips 1½″ × 8″ to the sides of the paper-pieced block, right sides together. Press the seam toward Fabric A.

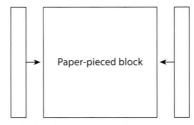

Add Fabric A strips to sides.

2 Sew the Fabric A rectangle 4½" × 10" to the bottom of the paper-pieced unit. Press the seam toward the rectangle.

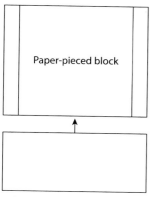

Add Fabric A rectangle to bottom.

3 Sew the Fabric B bib top to the top of the block unit, right sides together. Press the seam toward the bib top.

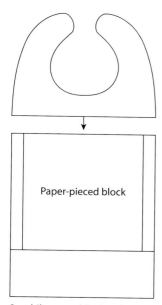

Sew bib top to block unit.

4 Remove remaining paper from the back of the paper-pieced block.

BIB LINING

1 Pin the bib front to the Fabric C lining, right sides together. Stitch ¼" from the edge of the bib front, leaving a 5" opening along one side of the bib.

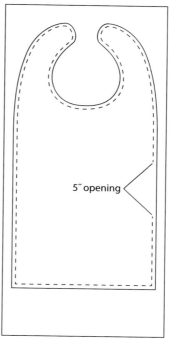

Stitch bib front to lining.

2 Trim the extra lining fabric, clip the curves, and turn the bib right side out. Press. Hand stitch the 5" opening closed. Topstitch ¼" away from the edge.

3 Quilt over the paper-pieced block through all thicknesses.

FINISHING

1 If your selected block requires buttons, appliqué felt circles in place at this time instead of buttons.

2 Fold up 2″ of the bib at the bottom to expose the lining on the front side. Stitch the lining flap to the bib in 3 places: ¼″ from both side edges, and down the center to form a crumb-catching pocket.

3 Stitch the male 1″ square of hook-and-loop tape to the lining side of the bib. Stitch the female 1″ square of hook-and-loop tape to the fabric side of the bib.

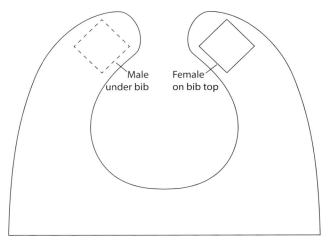

Male under bib   Female on bib top

Sew hook-and-loop tape to bib.

Stitch crumb-catching pocket in place.

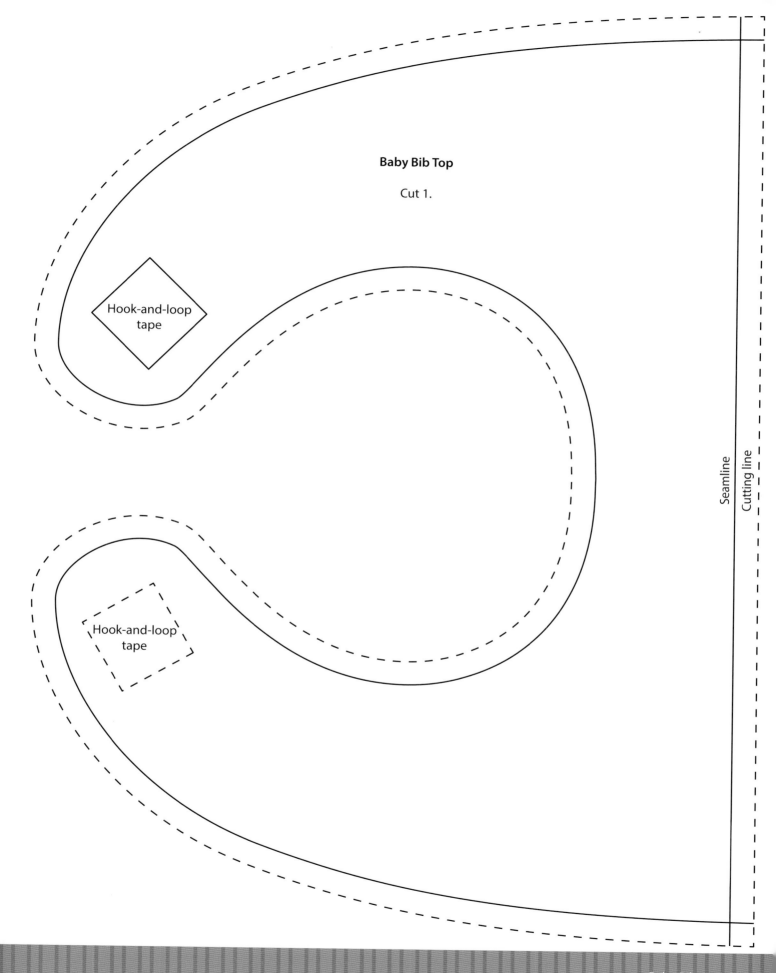

Baby Bib Top

Cut 1.

Hook-and-loop tape

Hook-and-loop tape

Seamline

Cutting line

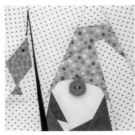

Block Patterns

REMEMBER …

- When making the blocks, refer to Paper-Piecing Basics (page 7) as needed.

- Any hand embroidery included in the following block instructions is meant to be done with foundation papers attached. (I use a running stitch or make French knots with 6 strands embroidery floss.)

- The specific project instructions will tell you when to remove foundation papers and attach buttons.

- The first fabric in the materials list is for the block background. If your project includes background fabric in its materials list, you can ignore the requirement listed for the block.

- *For baby's safety:* If your project is intended for a baby, whenever buttons are indicated in block patterns for eyes, substitute appliquéd felt circles in place of buttons.

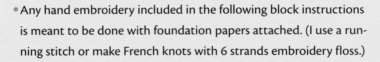

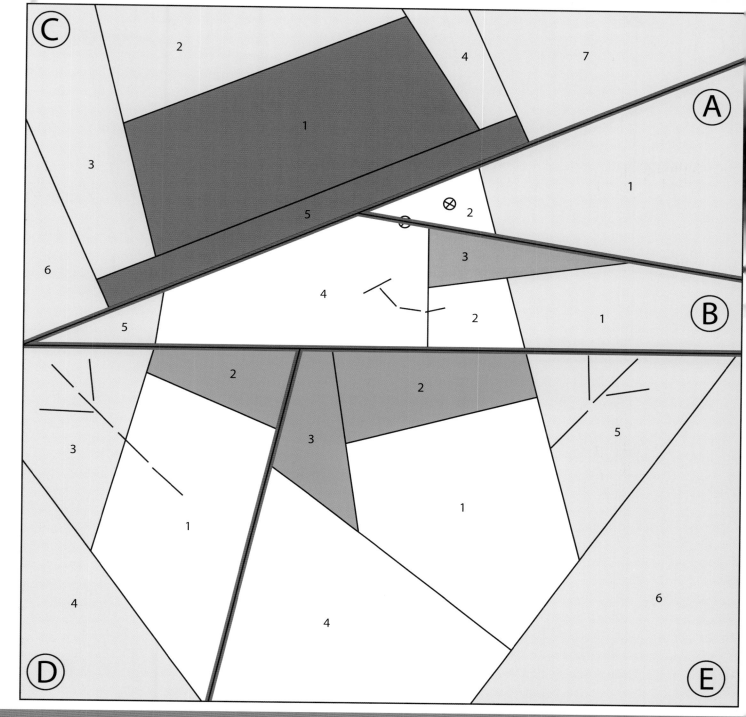

JANUARY, SNOWMAN 1

Materials

• Large scrap of blue, at least 9″ × 11″

• Scraps of white, orange, black, and green

• 2 black ⅛″ buttons for eyes

• Black embroidery floss

Directions

For detailed directions, refer to Paper-Piecing Basics (page 7).

1. Make 3 copies of the pattern (A/D, B, C/E).

2. Cut around each segment, adding ¼″ seam allowances at all red lines.

3. Paper piece each segment.

4. Connect the segments: A to B; A/B to C; D to E; A/B/C to D/E.

5. Trim the block to 8″ × 8″.

6. Hand stitch the mouth and the stick arms with a running stitch, using 6 strands of black embroidery floss.

7. Your project instructions will let you know when to hand stitch the button eyes in place, sewing through all thicknesses.

Block Patterns   **39**

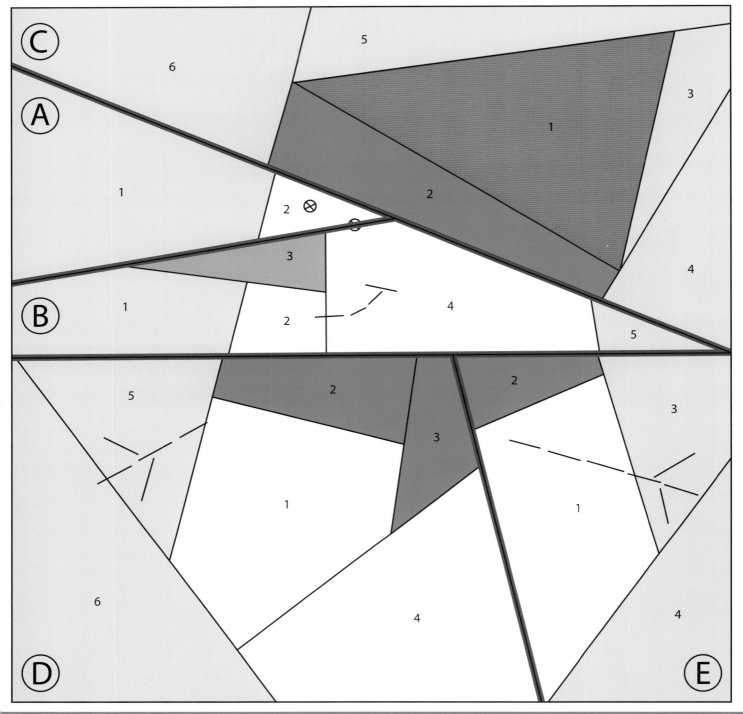

JANUARY, SNOWMAN 2

Materials

- Large scrap of blue, at least 9″ × 11″
- Scraps of white, orange, red, and green
- 2 black ⅛″ buttons for eyes
- Black embroidery floss

Directions

For detailed directions, refer to Paper-Piecing Basics (page 7).

1. Make 3 copies of the pattern (A/E, B, C/D).

2. Cut around each segment, adding ¼″ seam allowances at all red lines.

3. Paper piece each segment.

4. Connect the segments: A to B; A/B to C; D to E; A/B/C to D/E.

5. Trim the block to 8″ × 8″.

6. Hand stitch the mouth and the stick arms with a running stitch, using 6 strands of black embroidery floss.

7. Your project instructions will let you know when to hand stitch the button eyes in place, sewing through all thicknesses.

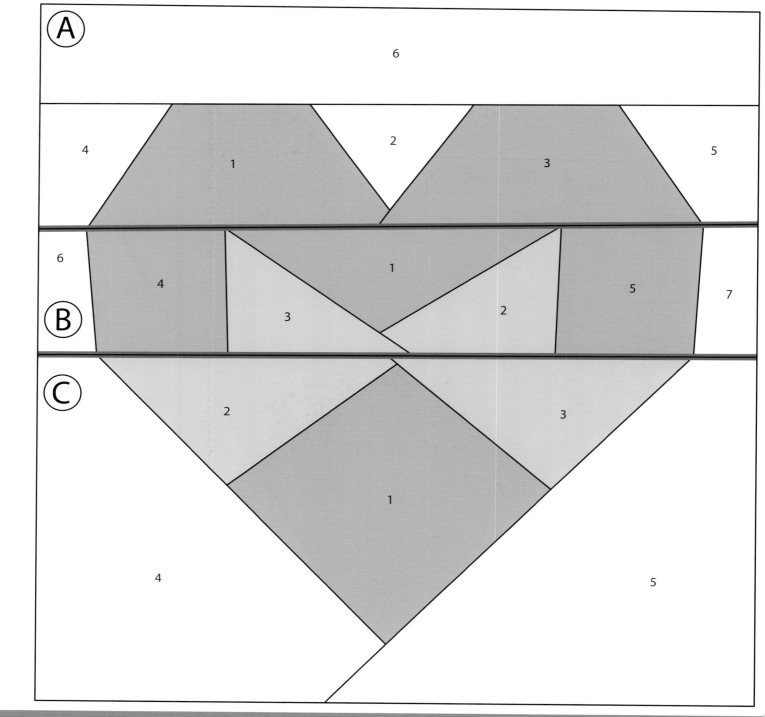

FEBRUARY, VALENTINE WITH BOW

Materials

- Large scrap of light pink print, at least 9″ × 11″
- Scraps of dark pink and blue

Directions

For detailed directions, refer to Paper-Piecing Basics (page 7).

1. Make 2 copies of the pattern (A/C, B).

2. Cut around each segment, adding ¼″ seam allowances at all red lines.

3. Paper piece each segment.

4. Connect the segments: A to B to C.

5. Trim the block to 8″ × 8″.

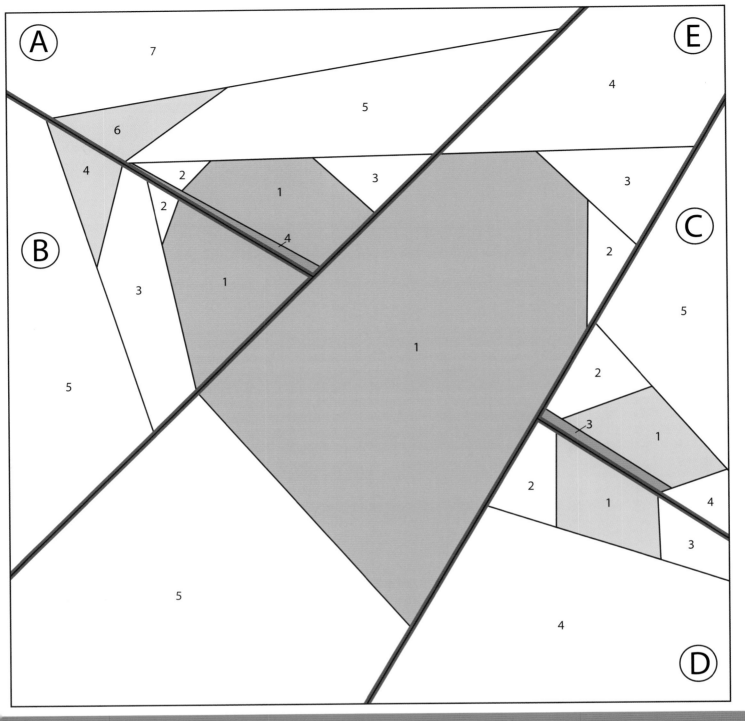

FEBRUARY, VALENTINE WITH ARROW

Materials
- Large scrap of light pink print, at least 9″ × 11″
- Scraps of dark pink, blue, and black

Directions
For detailed directions, refer to Paper-Piecing Basics (page 7).

1. Make 3 copies of the pattern (A/C, B/D, E).

2. Cut around each segment, adding ¼″ seam allowances at all red lines.

3. Paper piece each segment.

4. Connect the segments: A to B; C to D; A/B to E to C/D.

5. Trim the block to 8″ × 8″.

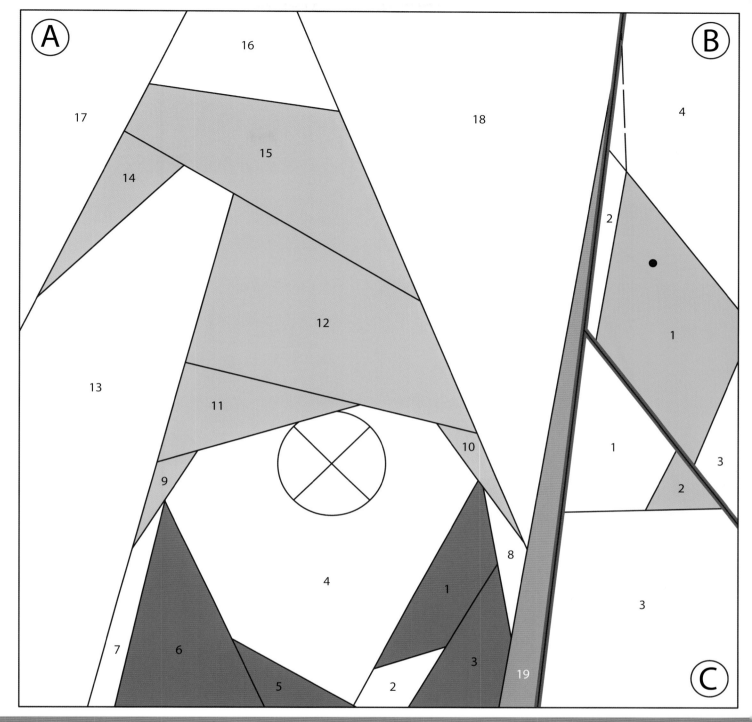

MARCH, GNOME WITH FISH

Materials

- Large scrap of white dot, at least 9″ × 11″
- Scraps of white, light blue, dark blue, black, and green
- 1 wooden 1⅛″ button for nose
- Black embroidery floss

Directions

For detailed directions, refer to Paper-Piecing Basics (page 7).

1. Make 3 copies of the pattern (A, B, C).

2. Cut around each segment, adding ¼″ seam allowances at all red lines.

3. Paper piece each segment.

4. Connect the segments: B to C; B/C to A.

5. Trim the block to 8″ × 8″.

6. Hand stitch the fishing line with a running stitch, and make a French knot for the fish eye, using 6 strands of black embroidery floss.

7. Your project instructions will let you know when to hand stitch the wooden button in place, sewing through all thicknesses.

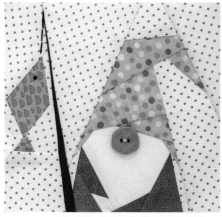

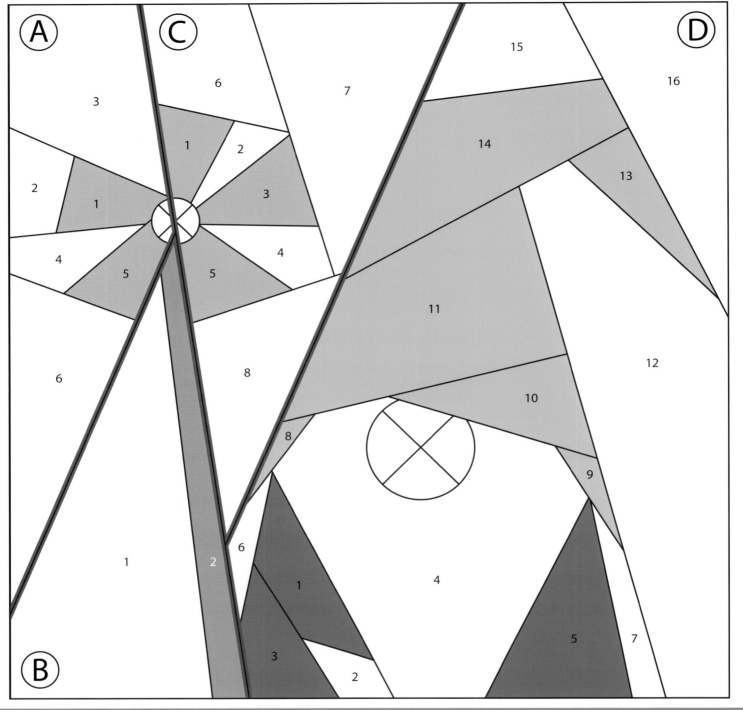

MARCH, GNOME WITH FLOWER

Materials

- Large scrap of white dot, at least 9″ × 11″
- Scraps of white, light blue, dark blue, black, and pink
- 1 wooden 1⅛″ button for nose
- 1 yellow ½″ button for flower center

Directions

For detailed directions, refer to Paper-Piecing Basics (page 7).

1. Make 3 copies of the pattern (A/D, B, C).

2. Cut around each segment, adding ¼″ seam allowances at all red lines.

3. Paper piece each segment.

4. Connect the segments: A to B; C to D; A/B to C/D.

5. Trim the block to 8″ × 8″.

6. Your project instructions will let you know when to hand stitch the buttons for the nose and the flower center in place, sewing through all thicknesses.

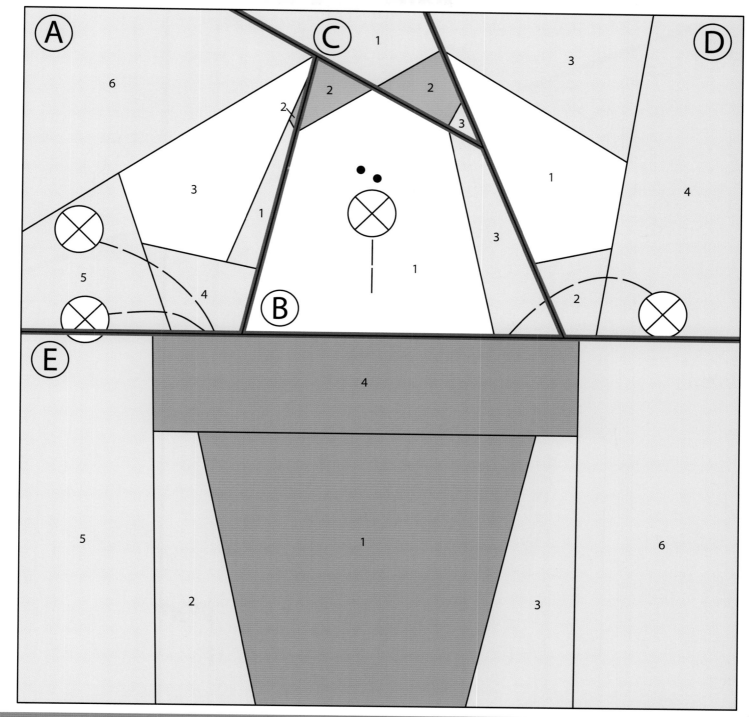

Materials

- Large scrap of blue, at least 9″ × 11″
- Scraps of white, brown, and pink
- 1 black ⅜″ button for nose
- 3 pink ½″ buttons for flowers
- Black embroidery floss

Directions

For detailed directions, refer to Paper-Piecing Basics (page 7).

1. Make 3 copies of the pattern (A/D, B, C/E).

2. Cut around each segment, adding ¼″ seam allowances at all red lines.

3. Paper piece each segment.

4. Connect the segments: A to B; A/B to C to D; A/B/C/D to E.

5. Trim the block to 8″ × 8″.

6. Hand stitch the flower stems and the mouth with a running stitch, and make French knot eyes, using 6 strands of black embroidery floss.

7. Your project instructions will let you know when to hand stitch the button for the nose and the flowers in place, sewing through all thicknesses.

Block Patterns **45**

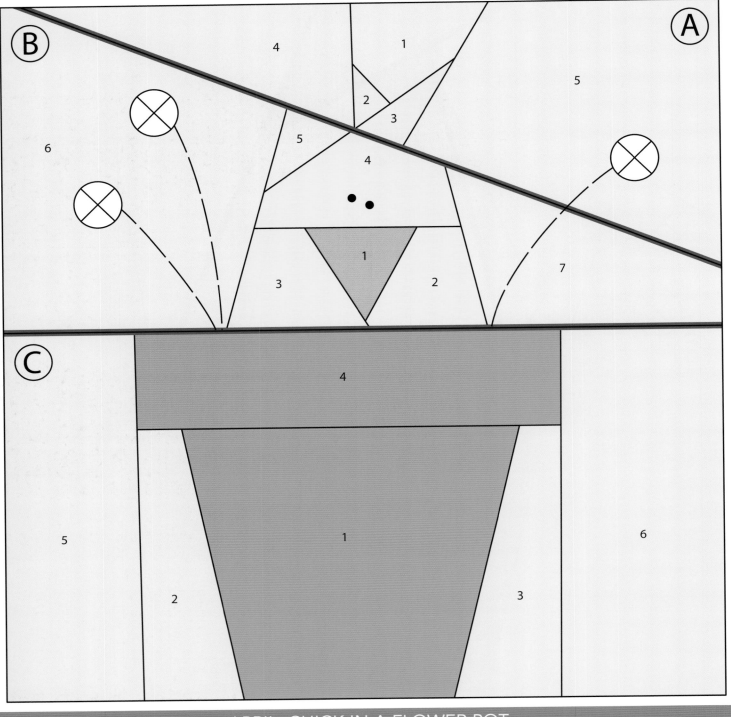

APRIL, CHICK IN A FLOWER POT

Materials

- Large scrap of blue, at least 9″ × 11″
- Scraps of yellow, orange, and brown
- 3 pink ½″ buttons for flowers
- Black embroidery floss

Directions

For detailed directions, refer to Paper-Piecing Basics (page 7).

1. Make 2 copies of the pattern (A/C, B).

2. Cut around each segment, adding ¼″ seam allowances at all red lines.

3. Paper piece each segment.

4. Connect the segments: A to B to C.

5. Trim the block to 8″ × 8″.

6. Hand stitch the flower stems with a running stitch, and make French knots for eyes, using 6 strands of black embroidery floss.

7. Your project instructions will let you know when to hand stitch the buttons for the flowers in place, sewing through all thicknesses.

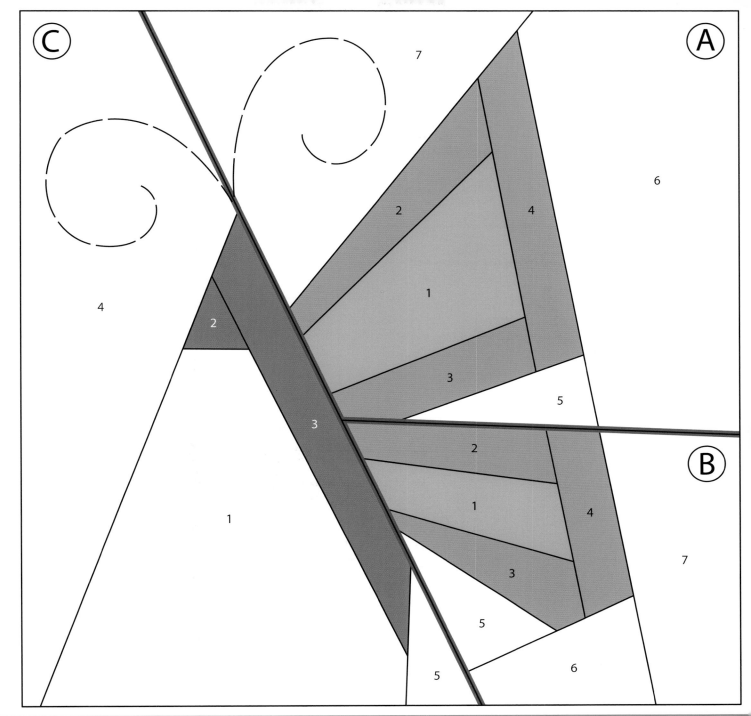

MAY, BUTTERFLY PROFILE

Materials
- Large scrap of white, at least 9″ × 11″
- Scraps of orange, solid black, and black print
- Black embroidery floss

Directions
For detailed directions, refer to Paper-Piecing Basics (page 7).

1. Make 3 copies of the pattern (A, B, C).

2. Cut around each segment, adding ¼″ seam allowances at all red lines.

3. Paper piece each segment.

4. Connect the segments: A to B; A/B to C.

5. Trim the block to 8″ × 8″.

6. Hand stitch the antennae with a running stitch, using 6 strands of black embroidery floss.

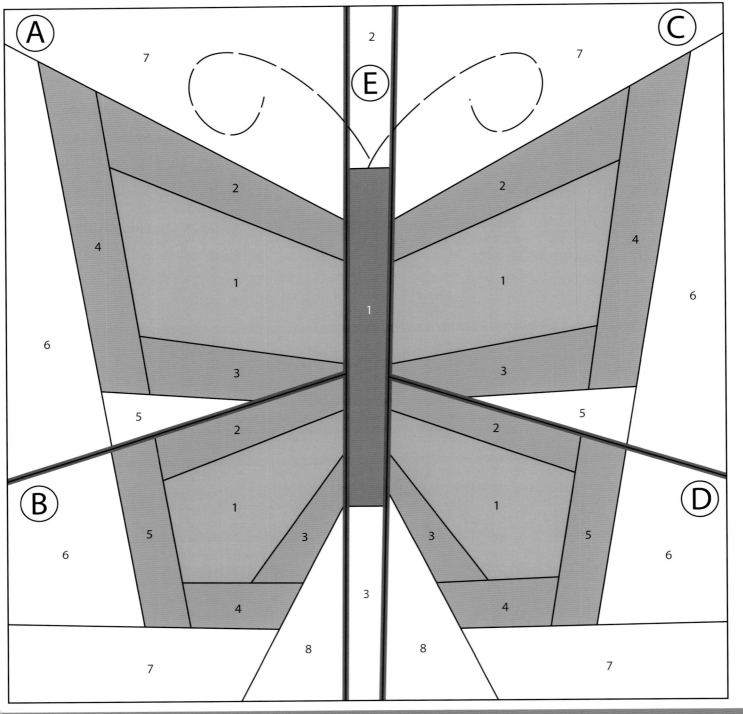

MAY, BUTTERFLY

Materials

- Large scrap of white, at least 9″ × 11″
- Scraps of orange, solid black, and black print
- Black embroidery floss

Directions

For detailed directions, refer to Paper-Piecing Basics (page 7).

1. Make 3 copies of the pattern (A/C, B/D, E).

2. Cut around each segment, adding ¼″ seam allowances at all red lines.

3. Paper piece each segment.

4. Connect the segments: A to B; C to D; A/B to E to C/D.

5. Trim the block to 8″ × 8″.

6. Hand stitch the antennae with a running stitch, using 6 strands of black embroidery floss.

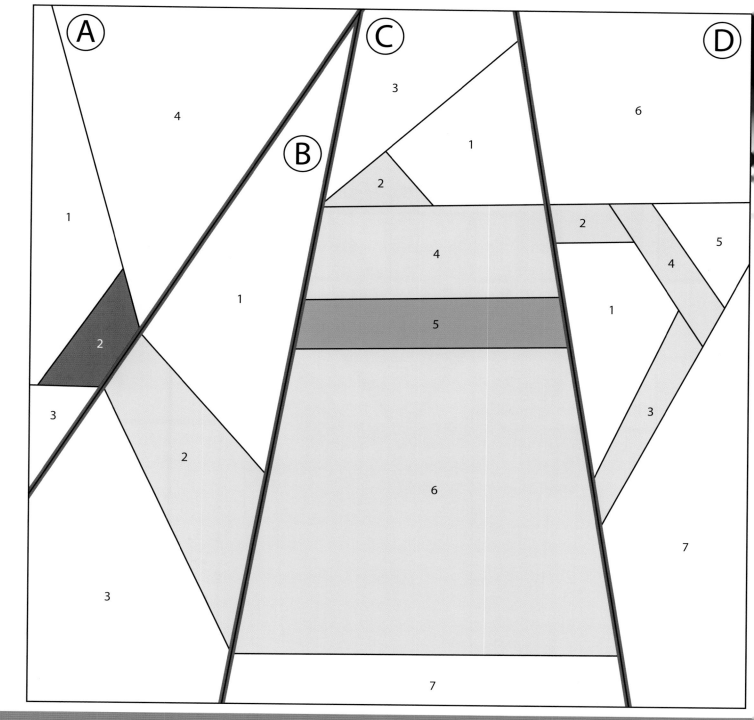

JUNE, WATERING CAN

Materials

- Large scrap of white, at least 9″ × 11″
- Scraps of light blue, dark blue, and black

Directions

For detailed directions, refer to Paper-Piecing Basics (page 7).

1. Make 3 copies of the pattern (A/D, B, C).

2. Cut around each segment, adding ¼″ seam allowances at all red lines.

3. Paper piece each segment.

4. Connect the segments: A to B; C to D; A/B to C/D.

5. Trim the block to 8″ × 8″.

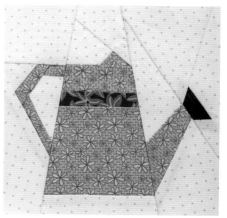

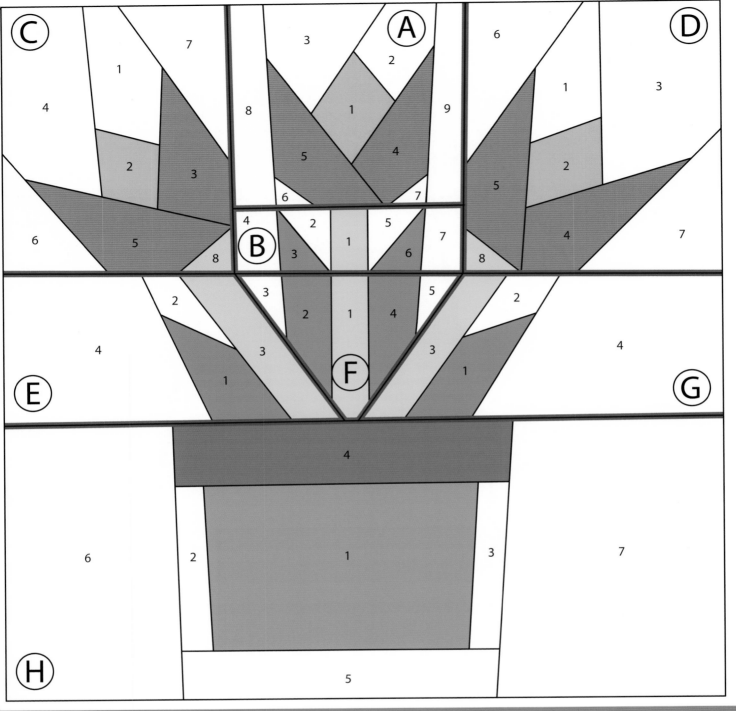

JUNE, TULIPS

Materials

- Large scrap of white, at least 9" × 11"
- Scraps of light pink, dark pink, light green, dark green, light blue, and dark blue

Directions

For detailed directions, refer to Paper-Piecing Basics (page 7).

1. Make 5 copies of the pattern (A/F, C/D, B/H, E, G).

2. Cut around each segment, adding ¼" seam allowances at all red lines.

3. Paper piece each segment.

4. Connect the segments: A to B; A/B to C to D; E to F to G; A/B/C/D to E/F/G to H.

5. Trim the block to 8" × 8".

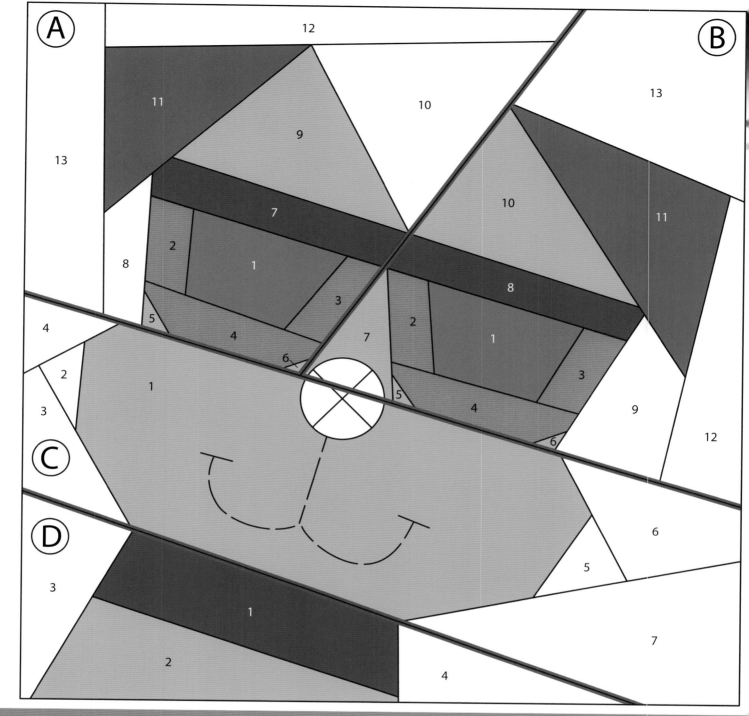

Materials

- Large scrap of white, at least 9″ × 11″
- Scraps of brown, dark brown, black, blue, and red
- 1 black ⅞″ button for nose
- Black embroidery floss

Directions

For detailed directions, refer to Paper-Piecing Basics (page 7).

1. Make 3 copies of the pattern (A/D, B, C).

2. Cut around each segment, adding ¼″ seam allowances at all red lines.

3. Paper piece each segment.

4. Connect the segments: A to B; A/B to C; A/B/C to D.

5. Trim the block to 8″ × 8″.

6. Hand stitch the mouth with a running stitch, using 6 strands of black embroidery floss.

7. Your project instructions will let you know when to hand stitch the button for the nose in place, sewing through all thicknesses.

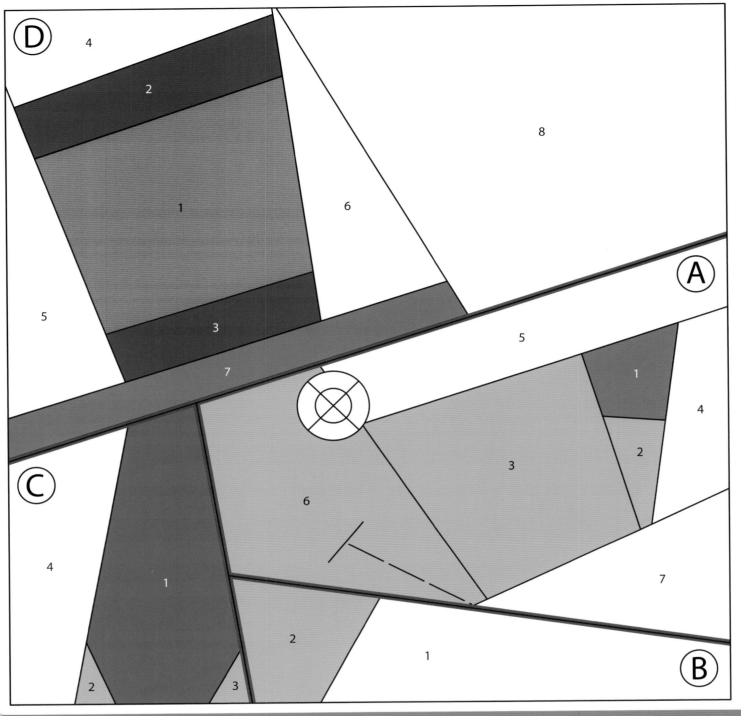

Materials

- Large scrap of white, at least 9″ × 11″
- Scraps of brown, dark brown, black, blue, dark blue, and red
- 1 white ¾″ button for eye
- 1 black ⅜″ button for eye pupil
- Black embroidery floss

Directions

For detailed directions, refer to Paper-Piecing Basics (page 7).

1. Make 3 copies of the pattern (A, B/D, C).

2. Cut around each segment, adding ¼″ seam allowances at all red lines.

3. Paper piece each segment.

4. Connect the segments: A to B; A/B to C; A/B/C to D.

5. Trim the block to 8″ × 8″.

6. Hand stitch the mouth with a running stitch, using 6 strands of black embroidery floss.

7. Your project instructions will let you know when to hand stitch the small button on top of the large button for the eye, sewing through all thicknesses.

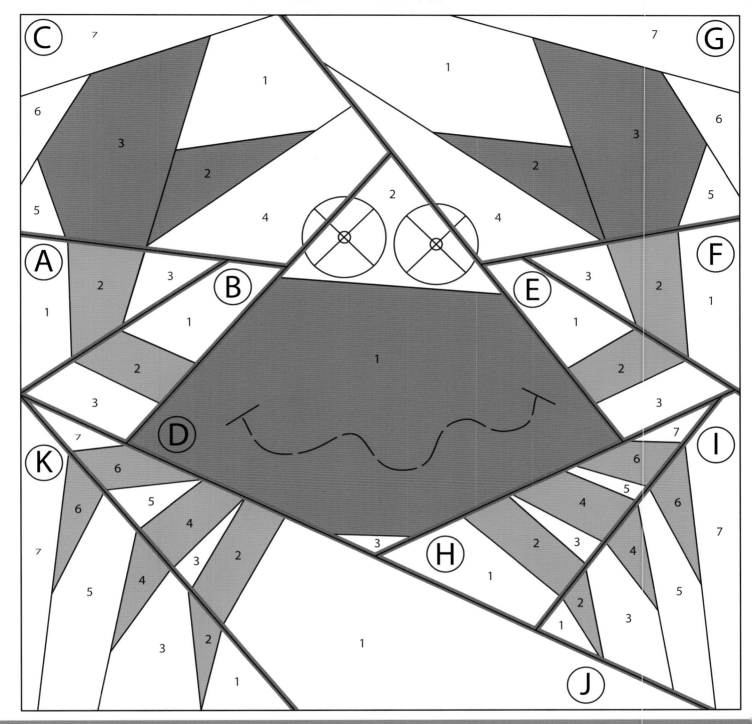

AUGUST, CRAB

Materials

- Large scrap of white, at least 9″ × 11″
- Scraps of red
- 2 black ⅞″ buttons for eyes
- 2 white ⅛″ buttons for eye pupils
- Black embroidery floss

Directions

For detailed directions, refer to Paper-Piecing Basics (page 7).

1. Make 5 copies of the pattern (A/E, C/J/F, B/G/I, K/H, D).

2. Cut around each segment, adding ¼″ seam allowances at all red lines.

3. Paper piece each segment.

4. Connect the segments: A to B; A/B to C; A/B/C to D; E to F; E/F to G; A/B/C/D to E/F/G; H to I; J to K; A–G to H/I; A–I to J/K.

5. Trim the block to 8″ × 8″.

6. Hand stitch the mouth with a running stitch, using 6 strands of black embroidery floss.

7. Your project instructions will let you know when to hand stitch the small white buttons on top of the large black buttons for the eyes, sewing through all thicknesses.

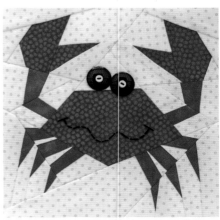

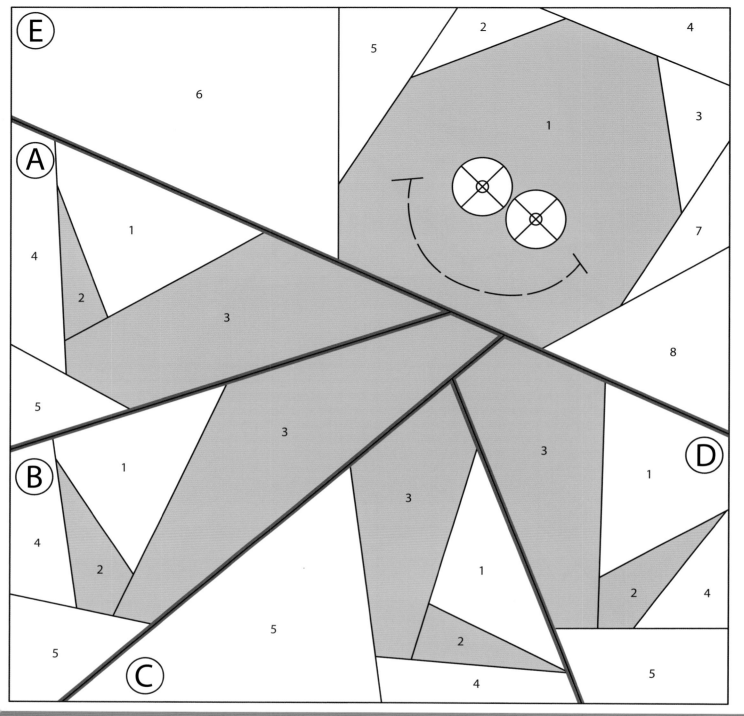

AUGUST, OCTOPUS

Materials

- Large scrap of white, at least 9″ × 11″
- Scraps of gray
- 2 white ⅝″ buttons for eyes
- 2 black ⅛″ buttons for eye pupils
- Black embroidery floss

Directions

For detailed directions, refer to Paper-Piecing Basics (page 7).

1. Make 4 copies of the pattern (A/C, B, D, E).

2. Cut around each segment, adding ¼″ seam allowances at all red lines.

3. Paper piece each segment.

4. Connect the segments: A to B; C to D; A/B to C/D; A/B/C/D to E.

5. Trim the block to 8″ × 8″.

6. Hand stitch the mouth with a running stitch, using 6 strands of black embroidery floss.

7. Your project instructions will let you know when to hand stitch the small black buttons on top of the large white buttons for the eyes, sewing through all thicknesses.

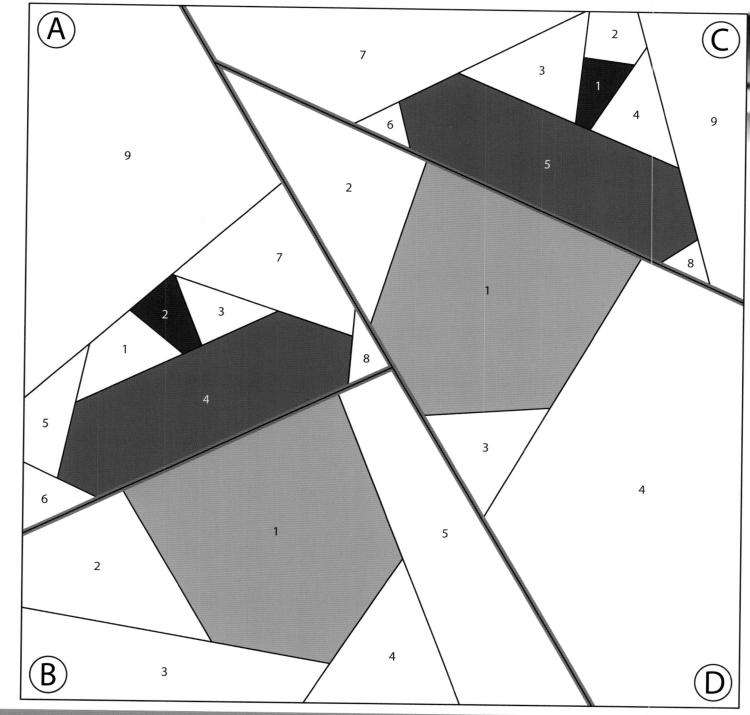

SEPTEMBER, ACORNS

Materials

- Large scrap of off-white, at least 9" × 11"
- Scraps of brown, dark brown, and solid dark brown

Directions

For detailed directions, refer to Paper-Piecing Basics (page 7).

1. Make 3 copies of the pattern (A, B/C, D).

2. Cut around each segment, adding ¼" seam allowances at all red lines.

3. Paper piece each segment.

4. Connect the segments: A to B; C to D; A/B to C/D.

5. Trim the block to 8" × 8".

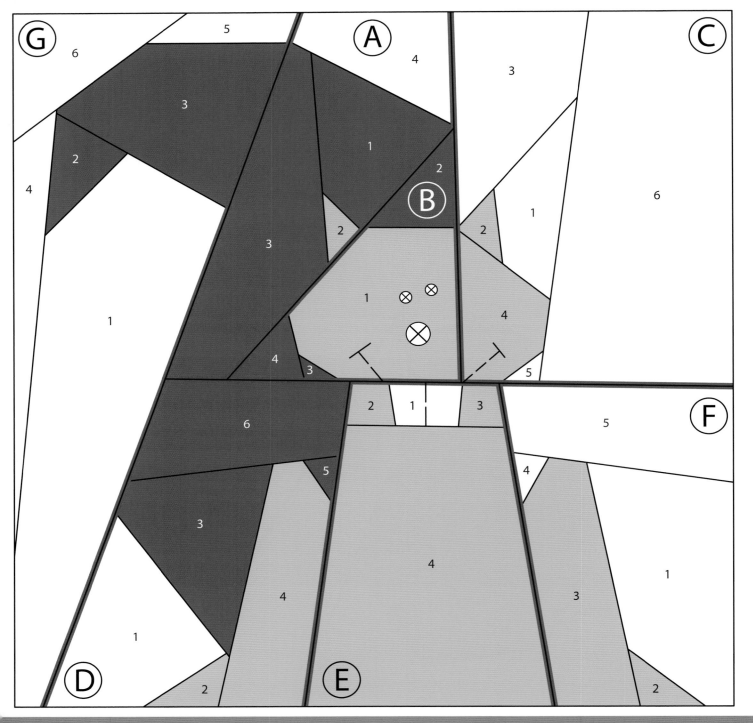

SEPTEMBER, SQUIRREL

Materials

- Large scrap of off-white, at least 9″ × 11″
- Scraps of white, brown, and dark brown
- 2 black ⅛″ buttons for eyes
- 1 black ¼″ button for nose
- Black embroidery floss

Directions

For detailed directions, refer to Paper-Piecing Basics (page 7).

1. Make 3 copies of the pattern (A/E, B/G/F, C/D).

2. Cut around each segment, adding ¼″ seam allowances at all red lines.

3. Paper piece each segment.

4. Connect the segments: A to B; A/B to C; D to E to F; A/B/C to D/E/F; A–F to G.

5. Trim the block to 8″ × 8″.

6. Hand stitch the mouth and line between the teeth with a running stitch, using 6 strands of black embroidery floss.

7. Your project instructions will let you know when to hand stitch the buttons for the eyes and nose in place, sewing through all thicknesses.

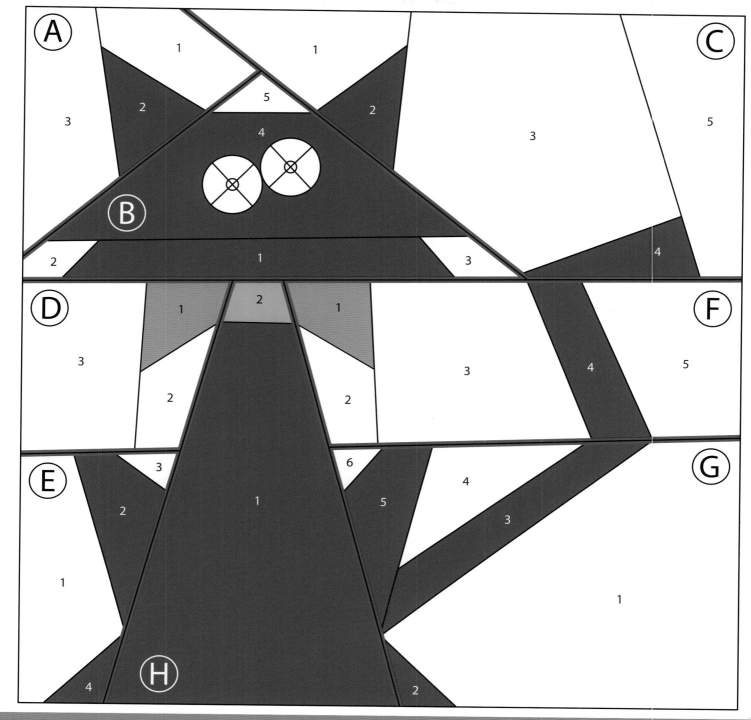

Materials

- Large scrap of white, at least 9″ × 11″
- Scraps of black, light orange, and dark orange
- 2 white ⅝″ buttons for eyes
- 2 black ⅛″ buttons for eye pupils

Directions

For detailed directions, refer to Paper-Piecing Basics (page 7).

1. Make 4 copies of the pattern (A/E/G, B, C/H, D/F).

2. Cut around each segment, adding ¼″ seam allowances at all red lines.

3. Paper piece each segment.

4. Connect the segments: A to B to C; D to E; F to G, D/E to H to F/G; A/B/C to D–H.

5. Trim the block to 8″ × 8″.

6. Your project instructions will let you know when to hand stitch the small buttons on top of the large buttons for the eyes, sewing through all thicknesses.

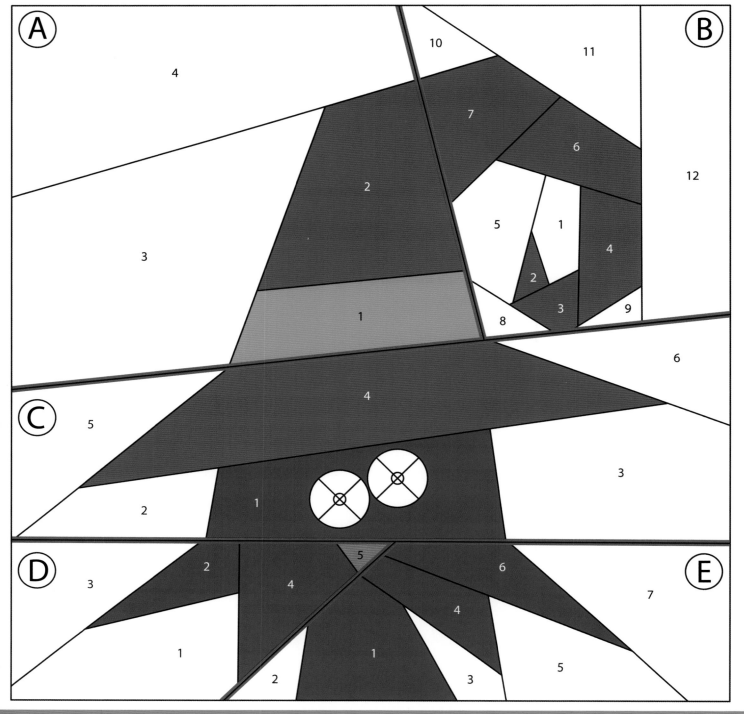

OCTOBER, CAT WITH HAT

Materials

- Large scrap of white, at least 9" × 11"
- Scraps of black, pink, purple, and orange
- 2 white ⅝" buttons for eyes
- 2 black ⅛" buttons for eye pupils

Directions

For detailed directions, refer to Paper-Piecing Basics (page 7).

1. Make 3 copies of the pattern (A/D, B/E, C).

2. Cut around each segment, adding ¼" seam allowances at all red lines.

3. Paper piece each segment.

4. Connect the segments: A to B; D to E; A/B to C to D/E.

5. Trim the block to 8" × 8".

6. Your project instructions will let you know when to hand stitch the small buttons on top of the large buttons for the eyes, sewing through all thicknesses.

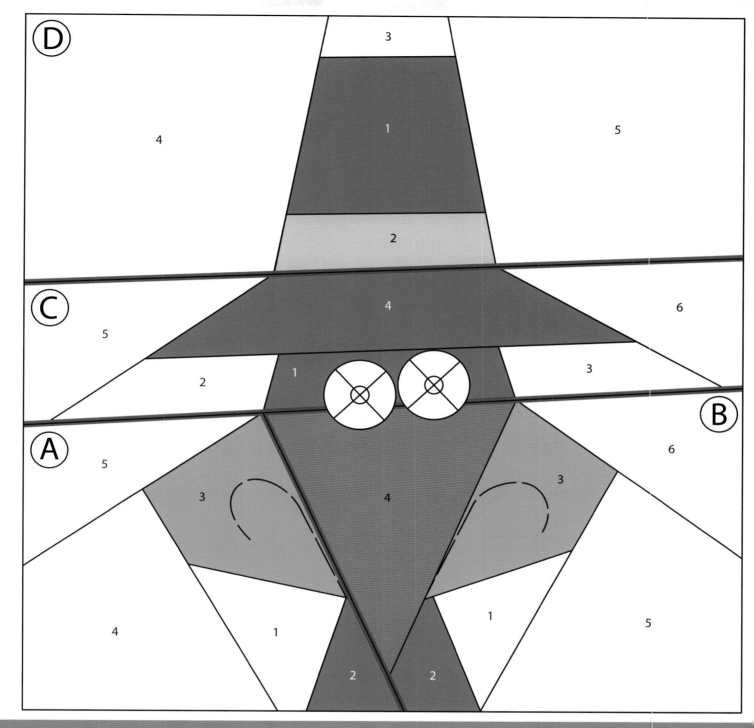

NOVEMBER, TURKEY WITH HAT

Materials

- Large scrap of off-white, at least 9″ × 11″
- Scraps of black, gold, light orange, dark orange, and brown
- 2 white ¾″ buttons for eyes
- 2 black ¼″ buttons for eye pupils
- Black embroidery floss

Directions

For detailed directions, refer to Paper-Piecing Basics (page 7).

1. Make 3 copies of the pattern (A/D, B, C).

2. Cut around each segment, adding ¼″ seam allowances at all red lines.

3. Paper piece each segment.

4. Connect the segments: A to B; A/B to C to D.

5. Trim the block to 8″ × 8″.

6. Hand stitch the mouth with a running stitch, using 6 strands of black embroidery floss.

7. Your project instructions will let you know when to hand stitch the small buttons on top of the large buttons for the eyes, sewing through all thicknesses.

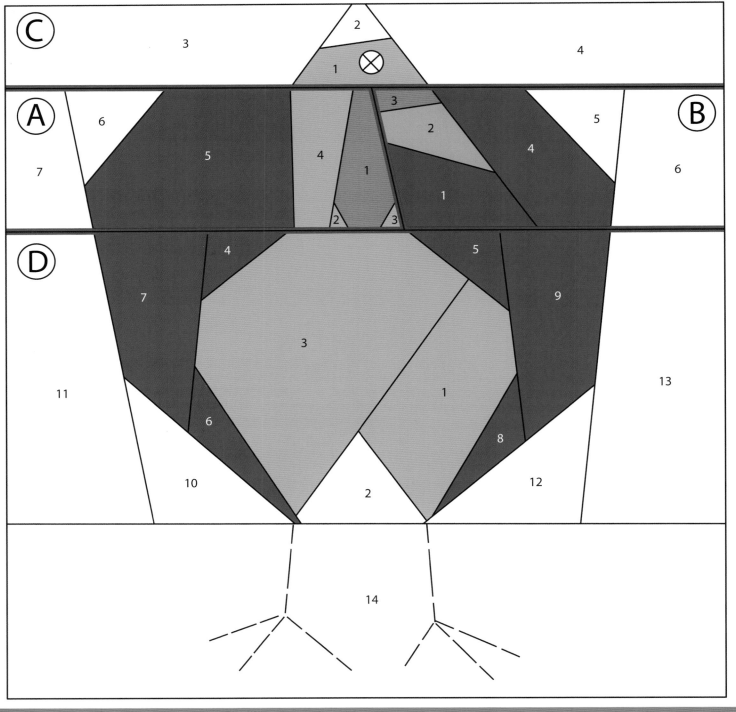

NOVEMBER, TURKEY

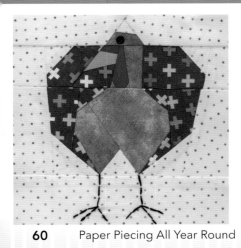

Materials

- Large scrap of off-white, at least 9″ × 11″
- Scraps of orange, red, brown and dark brown
- 1 black ¼″ button for eye
- Black embroidery floss

Directions

For detailed directions, refer to Paper-Piecing Basics (page 7).

1. Make 3 copies of the pattern (A, B, C/D).

2. Cut around each segment, adding ¼″ seam allowances at all red lines.

3. Paper piece each segment.

4. Connect the segments: A to B; A/B to C to D.

5. Trim the block to 8″ × 8″.

6. Hand stitch the legs and feet with a running stitch, using 6 strands of black embroidery floss.

7. Your project instructions will let you know when to hand stitch the button for the eye, sewing through all thicknesses.

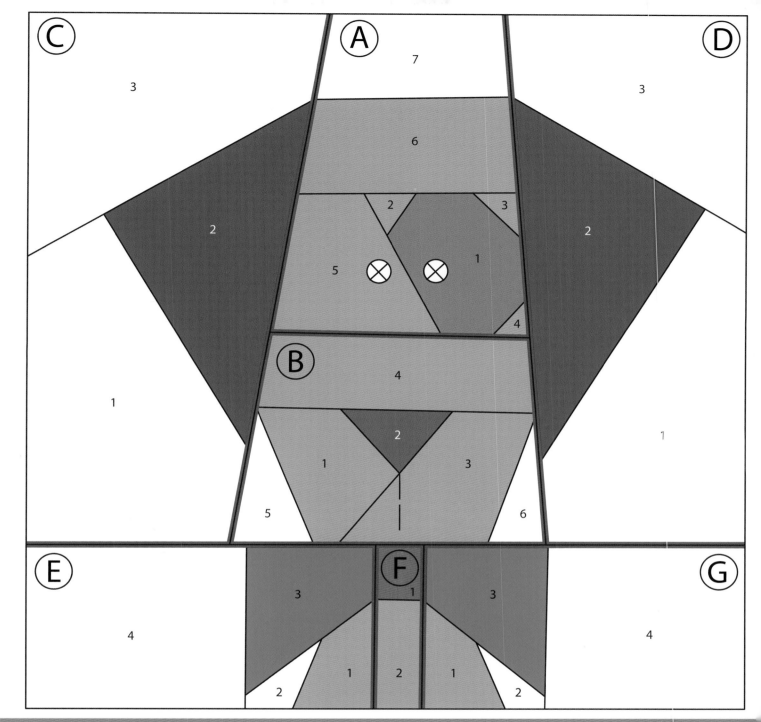

DECEMBER, CHRISTMAS PUPPY

Materials

• Large scrap of white, at least 9″ × 11″

• Scraps of brown, medium brown, dark brown, black, red, and green

• 2 black ¼″ buttons for eyes

• Black embroidery floss

Directions

For detailed directions, refer to Paper-Piecing Basics (page 7).

1. Make 3 copies of the pattern (C/D/F, A/E/G, B).

2. Cut around each segment, adding ¼″ seam allowances at all red lines.

3. Paper piece each segment.

4. Connect the segments: A to B; A/B to C to D; E to F to G; A/B/C/D to E/F/G.

5. Trim the block to 8″ × 8″.

6. Hand stitch the mouth with a running stitch, using 6 strands of black embroidery floss.

6. Your project instructions will let you know when to hand stitch the buttons for the eyes in place, sewing through all thicknesses.

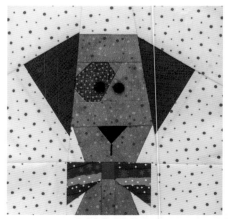

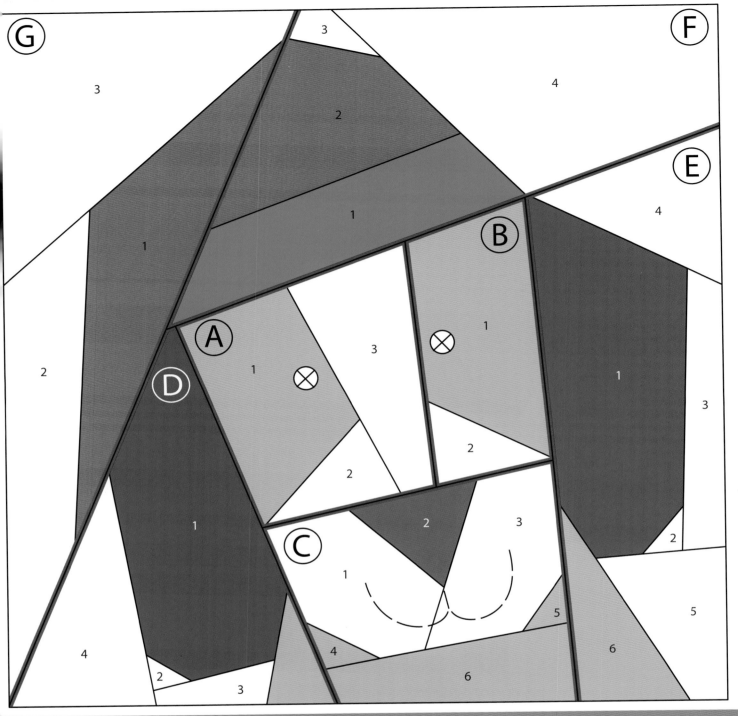

DECEMBER, CHRISTMAS PUPPY WITH HAT

Materials

- Large scrap of white, at least 9″ × 11″
- Scraps of white, brown, dark brown, black, red, and green
- 2 black ¼″ buttons for eyes
- Black embroidery floss

Directions

For detailed directions, refer to Paper-Piecing Basics (page 7).

1. Make 4 copies of the pattern (A/E, B/D, C/F, G).

2. Cut around each segment, adding ¼″ seam allowances at all red lines.

3. Paper piece each segment.

4. Connect the segments: A to B; A/B to C; A/B/C to D to E; A–E to F; A–F to G.

5. Trim the block to 8″ × 8″.

6. Hand stitch the mouth with a running stitch, using 6 strands of black embroidery floss.

7. Your project instructions will let you know when to hand stitch the buttons for the eyes in place, sewing through all thicknesses.

About the Author

Mary (also known as Marney) Hertel grew up on a small dairy farm in the heart of Wisconsin. Sewing is in her blood, and she likes to say she has "sewn since birth," starting on her mother's sewing machine at a very early age. After securing her art education job straight out of college, she used her first paycheck to purchase a sewing machine. Soon after, she started to quilt and has never stopped.

Mary's favorite method of quilting became paper piecing after she was introduced to this practice in 2013. The puzzle-like quality of paper piecing appealed to Mary and has quickly become her favorite approach to adding an image to a quilt.

Her quirky animal designs are a nod to 35 years of teaching children's art. "I try to keep my animal designs childlike, but expressive," Mary says. She also strives to offer her customers very easy paper-pieced patterns.

Currently, Mary has five previously published books, scores of magazine articles, and more than 200 patterns that can be found on Etsy.com, and in many quilting stores throughout the United States.

Enjoy her whimsical designs and her easy-to-paper-piece patterns.

Photo by Gail Cameron

Visit Mary online and follow on social media:

Website: madebymarney.com

Facebook: /madebymarney

Pinterest: /maryhertel

Instagram: @madebymarney

Twitter: madebymarney

Etsy: etsy.com/shop/madebymarney

Also by Mary Hertel: